# A Software Development Approach for Driving Competitiveness in Small Firms

The COVID-19 pandemic has forced many businesses to accelerate their digital transformation strategies to continue to meet the changing needs of their customers. This has resulted in significant growth in the global software market. However, for decades, managing software product quality has been a major challenge for many software development firms. This low success rate is due mainly to the development and delivery of low-quality software products. In addition to the direct costs associated with poor-quality software, software flaws can also raise security concerns, as hackers can gain complete control of various devices and data, such as mobile phones, computers, or the operational transactions of businesses. These security and privacy breaches are currently occurring with great frequency.

Although producers and consumers of software products spend vast amounts of money developing and purchasing these products, in many cases the promised benefits of user satisfaction, efficiency, productivity and profitability are not realized. In more severe circumstances, software development firms have failed and face the threat of going bankrupt, being acquired or suffering closure, because customers are demanding high-quality software products that they consistently fail to deliver. Small and medium enterprises (SMEs) operating within the software development industry have a more critical need to produce high-quality software since they are less able to absorb both the cost and the reputational impact of producing low-quality output.

*A Software Development Approach for Driving Competitiveness in Small Firms* provides some cost-efficient options that can help SMEs increase the likelihood that their software will be of high quality. It tells the story of the entrepreneurial journey that small firms should take to deliver high-quality software products. By utilizing practical examples and providing several recommended solutions to decrease the likelihood of producing low-quality software, the book outlines how mobilizing people, processes and technology are integral to the software development process and emphasizes why process maturity is the most influential factor in software development in small and medium enterprises.

# A Software Development Approach for Driving Competitiveness in Small Firms

Delroy A. Chevers

## CRC Press
Taylor & Francis Group
Boca Raton London New York

CRC Press is an imprint of the
Taylor & Francis Group, an **informa** business
AN AUERBACH BOOK

First edition published 2023
by CRC Press
6000 Broken Sound Parkway NW, Suite 300, Boca Raton, FL 33487-2742

and by CRC Press
4 Park Square, Milton Park, Abingdon, Oxon, OX14 4RN

*CRC Press is an imprint of Taylor & Francis Group, LLC*

ISBN: 978-1-032-43620-3 (hbk)
ISBN: 978-1-032-48417-4 (pbk)
ISBN: 978-1-003-38894-4 (ebk)

DOI: 10.1201/9781003388944

Typeset in Caslon
by SPi Technologies India Pvt Ltd (Straive)

# Contents

# Foreword

Dear Reader,

It has been my pleasure to know Dr Delroy A. Chevers since 2004 when we studied Information Systems at the University of the West Indies. Our interests had a common thread, Quality! IT Service Delivery and ITIL commanded my attention and my career pursuits include IT engineering (systems and networking) and consulting, production control operations and software quality assurance for large financial organization.

I recall us spending many hours debating current approaches in software development and the numerous studies on software quality and existing maturity models. Over the years we continued to discuss vigorously the merits of software process improvement (SPI) approaches and the value to be derived by organizations. However, our perspectives have increasingly diverged as we advance our careers towards academics, on the one hand, and industry, on the other.

Delroy has remained passionate about this area of Information Systems study and has written many valuable works with a focus on software development practices and information system quality among small firms in developing countries.

I've had the honour to review the work and arguments put forward in this publication, and I must say, not only has he provided a succinct version of his many previous works, but the book contains a new fresh perspective on earlier discussions on the applicability of existing SPI models in smaller organizations and furthers the need/ case for a modified framework. He outlines how mobilizing people, process and technology are integral to the software development process and emphasize why process maturity is the most influential factor in software development in small and medium enterprises.

I'm particularly blown away by Chapter 5 where he proposes a simplified software process improvement model for small firms (SPIM-S) based on their norms and constraints. I see this as a game changer as previous SPI models have easily overwhelmed small firms that typically possess limited resources, thus restricting their progress towards the delivery of high-quality software.

The author's motivation is to expose the fact that, although producers and consumers of software products spend vast amounts of money in developing and purchasing these products, in many cases the promised benefits of user satisfaction, efficiency, productivity and profitability are not realized. His book will provide you with a roadmap of the entrepreneurial journey that small firms should take to deliver high-quality software products.

This work is groundbreaking and is a credible reference for organizations in developing countries to utilize in pursuit of the lofty goals of producing quality software.

**G. Alex Campbell**
*Director, Systems Integration Engineering*

# Acknowledgements

I want to thank God most of all, for the inspiration, virtue and wisdom in the compilation of this book. I extend my gratitude to my wife, Jackie, for providing feedback on the drafts, as well as giving advice on the book cover. Special thanks to my mother, Cecelin, who always encourages me. To my daughter, Chevonnese, I say many thanks for creating all the graphic designs in the book. And thanks to my granddaughter, Arianna, for her understanding when grandpa was busy at the office and not being at home.

I am tremendously grateful to Professor Evan Duggan and Professor Annette Mills for their invaluable input and unwavering assistance and guidance through some challenging decisions. My friend, Mr Stanford Moore, intervened at the appropriate times to ensure that the compilation of the book was not as painful as it could have been and made the journey very intellectually rewarding. To my Fortis brother, Professor Chris Charles, my recent friend Professor Andrew Spencer and my colleague Dr Trevor Smith, I say thanks for the guidance regarding the book publishing process; I thank my classmates Mr Garfield Campbell and Mr Andrew Burke in reviewing the chapters; and Ms Deborah Fletcher, Ms Jonelle Allen, Ms Nordia Lawrence and Ms Maxine McDonnough for editing the book.

# About the Author

**Delroy A. Chevers** is a senior lecturer of Information Systems at the University of the West Indies, Mona. He holds a PhD in Information Systems from the University of the West Indies. He has over 25 years of experience in teaching and research. In 2019/2020, he received the Vice-Chancellor's Award for Excellence in Teaching at the University of the West Indies. In that same year, he received the Principal's Research Award for the Most Outstanding Researcher. In 2019, Delroy A. Chevers was appointed associate dean of Graduate Studies and Research in the Faculty of Social Sciences at the University of the West Indies. His research interests are Information Systems Quality and Success, and Project Management. He has published articles in top-tier international academic journals in Information Systems.

# Introduction

The COVID-19 pandemic has forced many businesses to accelerate their digital transformation strategies to continue to meet the changing needs of their customers. This has resulted in significant growth in the global software industry which is forecasted to grow at a rate of 11.7% annually up to 2030. With the advent of work-from-home and as consumers shift permanently to doing transactions and other activities such as learning online, innovative and creative technological methods are consistently being explored to deliver these truly digital propositions. This has led to an increased demand for software products.

However, for decades, managing software product quality has been a major challenge for many software development firms. In 2020, the total cost of poor software quality (CPSQ) in the US was US$2.08 trillion, with the largest contributors to CPSQ being operational software failures. This segment includes cybersecurity and software quality failures and cost businesses over US$1.56 trillion. One example of software quality failures is the technical coding errors in the software of the Boeing 737 that caused the death of 346 people in two crashes in 2018 and 2019 in Indonesia and Ethiopia, respectively. The next contributor to CPSQ other than cybersecurity was unsuccessful IT projects, which accounted for US$260 billion. According to the Standish Group, the success rate of software projects was 36%

in 2015. This low success rate is due mainly to the development and delivery of low-quality software products. In addition to the direct costs associated with poor quality software, software flaws can also create security concerns, where hackers can take complete control of various devices and data such as mobile phones, computers or firms' operational transactions. These security and privacy breaches are currently occurring at great frequency.

Although producers and consumers of software products spend vast amounts of money in developing and purchasing these products, in many cases the promised benefits of user satisfaction, efficiency, productivity and profitability are not realized. In more severe circumstances, software development firms have failed and face the threat of being bankrupt or acquired or suffer closure because customers are demanding high-quality software products which they consistently fail to deliver. Ashton-Tate Corporation founded in 1980 is one such company. The company was one of the 'Big Three' software development firms in the 1980s along with Microsoft and Lotus. Eventually, Ashton Tate was acquired in 1991, primarily because of software quality defects. Other examples are Polaroid Company which eventually filed for bankruptcy in 2001, Kodak Company which filed for bankruptcy in 2012 and Netscape Company which was acquired by America Online (AOL).

These failures can be reduced with the delivery of high-quality software products, and this book is meant to provide a streamlined approach to ensuring that software development companies produce high-quality software products. It is predicated on the main idea that people, process and technology are the major determinants in delivering high-quality software products. The ultimate strategy is to create an effective synergy of the right technology, skilled and committed people, along with a mature and well-understood process.

Small and medium enterprises (SMEs) operating within the software development industry have a more critical need to produce high-quality software since they are less able to absorb both the cost and reputational impact of producing low-quality output. The book, therefore, provides some cost-efficient options which can help SMEs to increase the likelihood that their software will be of high quality.

The post-COVID era has created a huge potential for SMEs in software development as firms continue to execute their digital transformation. The software market is also expected to benefit from the rising use of innovative technologies such as artificial intelligence (AI) and machine learning (ML), with software products such as those used in Enterprise resource planning (ERP) being increasingly demanded by firms to improve decision-making.

Individuals are also seeking more cost-efficient and secure software products, especially with the advent of work-from-home and the increase in online transactions. Consequently, software developers are forced to find creative, cost-effective ways to provide access to software products to these individuals. This desire has stimulated an increased demand for 'cloud-based' software products over 'on-premises' software products which are more expensive to maintain. The negative end-user experience as a result of poor software quality can lead to a reduction in sales which undermines the competitiveness and profitability of firms. This situation is particularly problematic for small firms that are unable to absorb such shocks, resulting in some of them going out of business.

This book tells the story of the entrepreneurial journey that small firms should take to deliver high-quality software products. By utilizing practical examples and providing several recommended solutions to decrease the likelihood of producing low-quality software, the book outlines how mobilizing people, process and technology are integral to the software development process and emphasize why process maturity is the most influential factor in software development in small and medium enterprises.

# THE CHALLENGES OF SOFTWARE DEVELOPMENT

The use of information technology (IT) has become pervasive in our daily lives, as well as in the management of organizations. It is impossible for either individuals or firms to operate and survive without technology. For individuals, it provides satisfaction in areas such as security, safety, communication and convenience. It allows organizations to be more productive and efficient, thereby achieving their strategic goals and gaining a competitive advantage. However, software is at the base of all the information technology advancements we see in our lives. Software is a collection of instructions that tell a computer how to work. An example of an antivirus software is Norton or McAfee.

A software is an intangible economic good, with no physical form (Kittlaus & Clough, 2009). Consequently, the functionality of software is generally perceptible through a user interface. Expressed differently, a software is any set of instructions that directs a computer processor to perform specific operations. Despite recent systematic approaches in software development, developers continue to face a number of challenges. There are times when incorrect instructions are given (called software failure/errors). Software failure occurs when the user perceives that the software has stopped delivering the expected result, with respect to the specification input values. The levels of failures can be classified on a continuum as catastrophic, critical, major, or minor.

## The Software Crisis – Software Errors

The literature is inundated with numerous software failures that have been catastrophic and critical. In 2020, the total cost of poor software quality (CPSQ) in the US was estimated at US$2.08 trillion

DOI: 10.1201/9781003388944-1

(Krasner, 2021). The largest contributor to CPSQ is operational failures, which includes cybersecurity failures and was estimated at US$1.56 trillion. This was followed by unsuccessful information technology projects at US$260 million. Poor software can cause a motor car to die or a smartphone to be hacked. Documented examples of software errors/flaws which have significantly affected companies, government and individuals (customers) are described below.

1. Technical coding errors in the software of the Boeing 737 caused the death of 346 people in two crashes in 2018 and 2019 in Indonesia and Ethiopia, respectively.
2. In May 2015, Airbus reported a software error in its A400M aircraft. This software error caused a fatal crash in Spain.
3. After stress testing the new baggage handling system at the Heathrow Terminal 5 in the UK, it was discovered on the go-live day of the project that the system could not cope with the real traffic of passengers and various nuances. This eventually led to the entire system being shut down, causing 42,000 bags to be transported without their owners and over 500 flights cancelled.
4. Israeli cybersecurity firm Sygnia exposed a global financial theft operation – the intruder software input fraudulent transactions in the host organization and then stole millions of dollars over time.
5. Soviet gas pipeline explosion – in June 1982, flaws in the programming of the software led to a massive explosion along parts of the pipeline, causing the largest non-nuclear explosion in the planet's history.
6. Ola, India's largest taxi aggregator, faced major security flaws within their system when software bugs helped basic programmers to enjoy unlimited free rides at the expense of Ola and users.
7. The Royal Bank of Scotland – in 2012, a failed upgrade to CA technology processing software by the Royal Bank of Scotland resulted in the breakdown of the system that affected millions of customers who were unable to access their accounts or execute payments.

8. The Canadian Government Services fell victim to two separate cyber-attacks in 2020 forcing some websites offline. These attacks compromised thousands of accounts relating to immigration services, employment and social resources. The attacks took advantage of the fact that many people reuse passwords and usernames across multiple accounts.

9. China has suspended Alibaba Cloud's services for six months after failing to report the serious internet bug which has put millions of systems and devices at hacking risk.

10. The Commonwealth Bank of Australia, the country's largest bank, was asked to explain why two software coding errors in its intelligent deposit machines found in 2016 were not reported until four years afterwards. The errors allowed the approval of personal overdrafts for 9,577 of its customers that should have been declined. In addition, another 1,152 customers received approvals for higher overdraft limits than they were qualified for.

11. In New Zealand in 2011, a computer glitch caused a free-for-all at Pak'n'Save after causing the doors to automatically open although the supermarket was officially closed. This software error allowed shoppers to walk away with free groceries during the period.

In summary, software failures can be costly, devastating and sometimes lead to loss of lives. Consequently, it is imperative that special care be taken by way of testing and quality assurance to ensure the attainment of the ISO/IEC software quality characteristics – functionality, maintainability, efficiency, reliability, usability and portability (Schulmeyer & McManus, 1999). The first two characteristics are known as internal quality attributes, and the remaining characteristics as external quality attributes. Internal quality is about the design of the software, while external quality is the fitness for purpose of the software. Compliance with these quality characteristics (whether internal or external attributes) can reduce the incidences of software failures. The occurrences of the stated software failures can negatively impact software products. These quality attributes will be explained further in the chapter.

Because software was earlier defined as being intangible, it begs the question, "what constitutes a software product?" A software product is defined, in this book, as a product whose primary component is software (Kittlaus & Clough, 2009). The failure of a car or the collapse of a bridge is similar to the failure of a software product, as these failures can range from minor to catastrophic.

Software products can be categorized in terms of the way the product is delivered to users (online or offline), according to its function (payment, communication, entertainment, etc.), or for whom it solves a problem (end customers or organizations). The latter classification is adopted in this book. It is important to share the difference between consumer (end customer) and business software products (government and organizations) because these examples will be used throughout the book. Some examples in each category are:

- Organizations:
    - Enterprise Resource Planning (ERP) Systems
    - AutoCAD
    - Google AdWords
    - Microsoft Office Suite
- Government:
    - Health Services
    - Revenue Management
    - Immigration Services
    - Social Services
    - Project Management
    - Microsoft Office Suite
- End customers (consumers):
    - Netflix
    - Games
    - Internet Banking
    - Google Search
    - Smartphones

Smartphones are so popular that they are now considered a major part of modern life. Although smart devices (software products) allow us to be constantly connected with each other, customers take for granted the huge difficulties that software development firms face in creating these products with all the requisite quality attributes, functionalities, privacy, security and safety features. Software quality is viewed as a strategic issue, so much so that a prominent software development firm in the US announced that it would pay rewards as high as US$200,000 to hackers who responsibly report crucial flaws in its software products (Perlroth, 2019).

Flaws in smartphone software are prevalent. In 2019, errors in smartphone tracking data prompted the review of 10,000 court verdicts in Denmark (Sorensen, 2019). This was a very serious internal quality failure in the software product which resulted in incorrect information and sending innocent people to prison. In another case reported in the *New York Times* article titled 'Apple was slow to act on the FaceTime bug that allowed spying on iPhones', a major security flaw was identified that exposed millions of iPhone users to eavesdropping (Perlroth, 2019). Using FaceTime, Apple's video chatting software, a caller could eavesdrop on the receiver's phone before the receiver had even answered the call. A bug so easy to exploit is every software company's worst security nightmare and every hacker, spy company, stalker and cybercriminal's dream. Vulnerabilities like these threaten not only personal privacy and safety but the security of nations (Quintin, 2018). These vulnerabilities are manifested in the stealing of a person's identity (identity theft), harassment, cyberextortion, data breach and bank fraud.

The occurrence of the stated software product failures can negatively impact the performance of software projects, causing time creep, budgetary overruns and software projects not realizing the intended specifications.

## The Software Crisis – Software Project Failures

In this book, a software project is defined as an environment of capable interrelated human resources managing a sequence of activities using appropriate methods and practices to develop a software product that conforms to customers' requirements (Zeineddine & Mansour, 2005). Software projects take into account the entire software development process which ranges from requirement gathering to testing and maintenance. A misstep in the execution of a software project can lead to significant failures.

For decades, managing software product quality has been a major challenge for many software development firms (Chevers et al., 2020). Individuals and firms have been spending a huge amount of capital and a vast amount of time in the purchasing and implementation of software products. Yet, they have not been able to reap the promised benefits of satisfaction, efficiency and productivity. In some instances, firms have failed, faced the threat of bankruptcy and acquisition, or suffered closure because customers are demanding high-quality software products. The Ashton-Tate Corporation, founded in 1980, was one of the 'Big Three' software development firms, which included Microsoft and Lotus. Eventually, the company was acquired in 1991 primarily because of software quality defects. Other examples are the Polaroid Company that eventually filed for bankruptcy in 2001, Kodak Company that filed for bankruptcy in 2012, and Netscape Company that was acquired by America Online (AOL).

The Standish Group is an independent international information technology (IT) research firm that is known for its reports on the success and failure rates of software projects. The 2015 Chaos Report on software project success shows the rate of success being 29%, challenged projects at 52% and failed projects at 19% (Standish Group, 2015).

Successful projects are those projects that are delivered on time, on budget and with required features and functionalities. Challenged projects are those that are late, over budget and/or with less than the required features and functions, while failed projects are those that are cancelled prior to completion or delivered but never used (Standish Group, 2015).

The information systems (IS) community has not effectively exploited the strides made in the information technology discipline, and as such has not been able to produce high-quality software products with consistency (Dwivedi et al., 2014). This phenomenon has been labelled the 'Software crisis' (Brynjolfsson, 1993; Gibbs, 1994). The problem of a software crisis was first mentioned by Gladden (1982), when he referred to the problems of software being delivered over time, over budget and with limited functionalities. Since then, many persons have supported this claim and have highlighted a variety of ways in which the crisis manifests itself from the 1980s to present. Some of the problems are outlined below.

- There are no 'Silver bullets' to slay the software werewolf.
- Seventy-five percent of software development projects are never completed or remain unused.
- Software delivery quality is one of the top ten IS management problems.
- Software projects are notorious for scope changes, escalation and abandonment.
- About 50% of IS executives are dissatisfied with the quality of their organization's software products.
- Only 24% of software projects in *Fortune* 500 companies are successful.
- There is a high degree of uncertainty and volatility in software projects.
- Only 29% of software projects are successful.

These challenges have plagued the IS community for decades, yet it is widely accepted that there is no 'Silver bullet' to slay the software werewolf (Brooks, 1987). In fact, some persons believe that 'Silver pellets' are required to gradually chip away at the 'monster' of the software crisis.

## Software Quality

Software users are currently demanding higher quality software products than ever before. And these users are willing to pay premium prices for high-quality software products (Wong, 2006). However, software products can be error-ridden, due mainly to the growing complexity of the software development and delivery process (Hossain, 2018). It is estimated that software developers usually spend about 80% of the development costs on identifying and correcting defects/bugs, yet software products are delivered with bugs (Hossain, 2018). The failure of software products costs the US economy approximately $59.5 billion annually or about 0.6% of the gross domestic product (Tassey, 2002). Software testing is the main means of detecting and resolving bugs, whether by humans or software development tools or both. This approach will be explored further in Chapter 2.

To develop software products on time (quickly) and within budget is useless if the product delivered is full of defects/bugs. It is important to note that the cost of fixing bugs increases along the software development cycle, from requirement analysis to evolution/mainte-nance (Wong, 2006). The cost of correcting bugs in software products late in the development cycle can be multiple times greater than the cost of correcting them at the early stages. This cost can be extremely high if the bug is discovered after delivery to the customer. It is imperative that a policy of preventing defects is employed at all times. During the evolution from the analog to the digital smart phone, it is critical that the requirements of customers/users are captured and incorporated in the design of the phones. Some of the features are internet connectivity, a mobile browser, wireless synchronization with other devices such as laptop or desktop computers and a strong pro-cessor. These features need to be functional and working at all times because customers are demanding the 'always on' mode in which everything is at their fingertips and working properly, as well as being ubiquitous in which they want to be everywhere at the same time.

Figure 1.1 shows the software development life cycle in which there is requirement analysis, followed by design, then implemen-tation, during which there is software testing and finally evolution/ maintenance. Some of the activities undertaken along the cycle are the identification of individuals and business problems, identification of opportunities via technology, establishment of specific and measur-able objectives, determination of user/business requirements, analysis of user needs, design of the recommended software product, devel-opment of the software product, documentation of the relevant pro-cesses and practices, testing the proposed software product, deploying and maintaining the final software product, and evaluating the qual-ity characteristics of the software product. A widely held criticism of

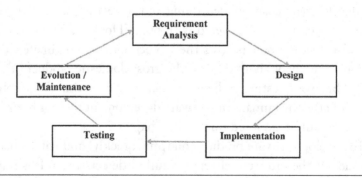

**Figure 1.1**   The software development life cycle.

the cycle is the long gestation period required for a project to move from requirement analysis to evolution/maintenance, but the goal is to deliver a high-quality software product at the end of the cycle.

Quality can only be achieved when there is a sense of what the term 'quality' really means; only then can it be measured. Quality is a complex and multifaceted concept, but in the software product the simplest sense of product quality is a lack of 'bugs'. Consequently, quality software is defined by the extent to which a defined set of desirable features is incorporated into a product so as to enhance its lifetime performance (Fitzpatrick, 1996). A high-quality software product is defined as a product that reliably produces required features that are relatively easy to access and use (Duggan, 2003). In this book, quality software is seen as an array of features or characteristics of a software product that represent its ability to satisfy stated or implied needs. In essence, software quality is the extent to which quality characteristics are designed and incorporated into a software product or service. Some of these desirable features or quality characteristics, as shown in Figure 1.2, are functionality, maintainability, efficiency, reliability, usability and portability (ISO, 1991).

A quality product does exactly what the user wants it to do. Hence, a useful way to discuss quality is in relation to user/customer satisfaction, which can be measured in terms of:

- the features and characteristics of the software product; and
- the absence of defects in the software product.

These two characteristics encapsulate what is commonly referred to as 'quality of design', which includes functionality and maintainability.

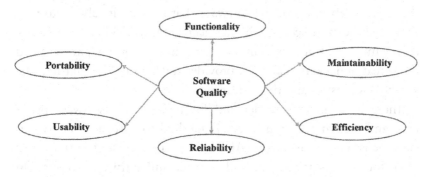

**Figure 1.2**   ISO_IEC quality characteristics.

**Table 1.1**    Definition of the Quality Characteristics

| QUALITY CHARACTERISTICS | DEFINITION |
|---|---|
| QUALITY OF DESIGN | |
| Functionality | Extent to which the software product conforms to its specifications and conforms to its declared objectives |
| Maintainability | Ease of effort for locating and fixing a software product failure within a specified time period |
| QUALITY OF PERFORMANCE | |
| Efficiency | Extent to which the software product is able to do more with less resources |
| Reliability | Extent to which the software product will perform within a specified time period |
| Usability | Relative ease of learning and the operation of the software product |
| QUALITY OF ADAPTATION | |
| Portability | Ease of effort to transport the software product to another environment and/or platform |

Table 1.1 lists the six quality characteristics in three broad categories of 'quality of design', 'quality of performance' and 'quality of adaptation', as well as provides their definition.

Quality is the customer's perceived value of the software product, which can be subjective. So, in an attempt to objectively measure the quality characteristics, various sub-characteristics are associated with each characteristic. For example, two of the five sub-characteristics for functionality are suitability and security. The suitability sub-characteristic is concerned with the quality attributes of the software product that relate to the presence and appropriateness of a set of functions for specified tasks, while security is concerned with the quality attributes of the software that bear on its ability to prevent unauthorized access, whether accidental or deliberate. Security is very important in these times of E-commerce, online payment and the threat of hackers. Table 1.2 provides further details regarding the sub-characteristics and their meaning.

There is an increasing demand for high-quality software products, and applying a high level of standard to software quality can ensure customer satisfaction (Al Obisat et al., 2018). The attainment of customer satisfaction can lead to successful software projects. On the contrary, poor software quality has been responsible for business

**Table 1.2**    ISO/IEC Quality Characteristics and Their Sub-Characteristics

| QUALITY CHARACTERISTICS | SUB-CHARACTERISTICS | MEANING |
|---|---|---|
| Functionality | Are the required functions available in the software product? | |
| | Suitability | Attributes of the software product that relate to the presence and appropriateness of a set of functions for specific tasks |
| | Security | Attributes of software product that relate to its ability to prevent unauthorized access, whether accidental or deliberate |
| | Accuracy | Attributes of software product that relate to the provision of right or agreed results or efforts |
| | Interoperability | Attributes of software product that relate to its ability to interact with specified systems |
| | Compliance | Attributes of software product that make the software adhere to application-related standards or conventions or regulations in laws and similar prescriptions |
| Maintainability | How easy is it to modify the software product? | |
| | Stability | Attributes of software product that relate to the risk of unexpected effect of modifications |
| | Analysability | Attributes of software product that relate to the effort needed for diagnosis of deficiencies or cases of failures, or for identification of parts to be modified |
| | Changeability | Attributes of software product that relate to the effort needed for modification, fault removal or for environmental change |
| | Testability | Attributes of software product that relate to the effort needed for validating the modified software |
| Efficiency | How efficient is the software product? | |
| | Time behaviour | Attributes of software product that relate to response and processing times and on throughput rates in performing its function |
| | Resource behaviour | Attributes of software product that relate to the amount of resources used and the duration of such use in performing its function |
| Reliability | How reliable is the software product? | |
| | Maturity | Attributes of software product that relate to the frequency of failure by faults in the software |
| | Recoverability | Attributes of the software that relate to the capacity to re-establish its level of performance and recover the data directly affected in case of a failure and on the time and effort needed for it |
| | Fault tolerance | Attributes of software product that relate to its ability to maintain a specified level of performance in case of software faults or of infringement of its specified interface |

*(Continued)*

**Table 1.2**   (Continued)

| QUALITY CHARACTERISTICS | SUB-CHARACTERISTICS | MEANING |
|---|---|---|
| Usability | Is the software product easy to use? | |
| | Learnability | Attributes of the software product that relate to the user's effort for learning its application |
| | Understandability | Attributes of software product that relate to the user's effort for recognizing the logical concept and its applicability |
| | Operability | Attributes of software products that relate to the user's effort for operation and operation control |
| Portability | How easy is it to transfer the software product to another environment? | |
| | Installability | Attributes of software products that relate to the effort needed to install the software in a specified environment |
| | Conformance | Attributes of software products that make the software adhere to standards or conventions relating to portability |
| | Replaceability | Attributes of a software products that relate to opportunity and effort of using it in the place of other specified software in the environment of the software |
| | Adaptability | Attributes of a software product that relate to the opportunity for its adaptation to different specified environments without applying other actions or means than those provided for this purpose for the software considered |

failures, severe safety disasters and serious security issues (Carrozza et al., 2018). As a result, quality must be defined and measured in an effort to seek quality improvement and successful projects.

## Software Production Methods

In response to the software crisis, several software production methods have been tried to ameliorate the problem of delivering low-quality software products. There are four major software development methods that have evolved over the years (Duggan, 2006). These are the traditional waterfall model, user-centred, reuse-based and incremental/iterative as shown in Figure 1.3. The purpose of the evolution of these production methods is to increase the quality of the delivered software product, as well as enhance quick-to-market, which is a strategic move to get high-quality software product to the consumer

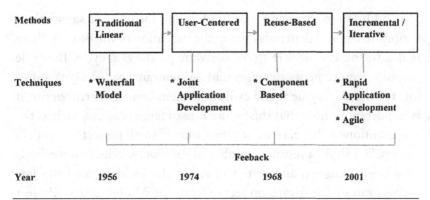

| Methods | Traditional Linear | User-Centered | Reuse-Based | Incremental / Iterative |
|---|---|---|---|---|
| Techniques | * Waterfall Model | * Joint Application Development | * Component Based | * Rapid Application Development * Agile |
| | | | Feeback | |
| Year | 1956 | 1974 | 1968 | 2001 |

**Figure 1.3**   Software production methods.

before the competitor. Such strategic moves can provide a competitive advantage. To gain competitive advantage over its rivals, a company must perform its activities in a way that leads to differentiation in terms of quality dimensions, customer satisfaction and price (Porter & Millar, 1985).

Both developed and developing economies can adopt all or any of these production methods. Hence, these methods do not present a major divide in developed versus developing economies, nor do they present a divide between large and small firms, but if adopted they can offer an opportunity to increase the likelihood of delivering high-quality software products.

Software development is a complex and innovative process (Anees & Agrwal, 2017). Firms usually respond to business challenges with computer-based information systems (Laudon & Laudon, 2015). For example, increased demand from customers for lower prices, as well as increased rivalry in the retail industry, might force a department store to adopt the competitive priority of providing low prices to its customers every day. To achieve this goal, the operations strategy employed could be low inventory levels, facilitated by linking the communication among all stores countrywide. The enabling technology to link all the stores might be electronic data interchange (EDI). A software project of this magnitude is complex and involves many key stakeholders. The stakeholders of such projects might include as the project sponsor (budget holder), project steering committee, system analysts, developers, network administrators, interface design experts, database administrators, users of the delivered system and customers.

In addition to the many stakeholders and the quest to satisfy their various needs and demands during the execution of the project, there is also the need to adhere to the software production cycle. The cycle involves requirements management, system analysis, design, sourcing, testing, deployment and evolution/maintenance. Furthermore, it is important to note that the failure rate of large projects, such as the one mentioned above, is higher than that of small projects (Standish Group, 2015). As a result, a number of software production methods have been designed and tested to arrest the incidences of the low success rates of software projects (Joslin & Muller, 2016). Project size is classified as small, medium and large based on the number of team members, with small having less than 16 members, medium having 16–45 members, and large having over 45 members (Kabore et al., 2021).

### The Tradition Linear Sequential Method – The Waterfall Model

The waterfall model is the oldest software production method. It was created in 1956 to provide a structured approach to software development. This approach underscores that the amount of time spent early in the software production cycle can reduce costs at later stages. Instead, the waterfall model attributes equal focus on each project activity and assigns a linear, sequential approach to each phase of the project. It dictates that each phase in the development process begin only after the previous phase is reviewed, verified and completed. Hence, the waterfall model is classified as a plan-driven approach in software development. The benefits of this production method, as stated by Alshamrani and Bahattab (2015) and Kramer (2018), are:

- simple and easy to understand and implement;
- widely used and known;
- provides a structure for organizing and controlling a software development project;
- works well where requirements are well understood by key stakeholders;
- easy to manage due to the rigidity of the model;
- determines the end goal at the early state of the development cycle in which software developers seek the requirements of users during the analysis stage of the cycle;

- well understood milestones;
- easy to arrange tasks;
- delays testing until after project completion; and
- makes scope changes difficult.

This development approach was borrowed from the engineering discipline, which realizes project success through a series of structured and ordered steps. Because there are set ways to successfully design and build things like bridges, houses and cars, it was felt that the same method could be applied to software development with equal levels of success. This approach starts with requirements management, analysis, design, implementation, testing and deployment and ends with maintenance, as shown in Figure 1.4. There are a fixed number of steps to be taken in a particular order (like a recipe).

Engineering development tends to be less iterative and flexible, as progress flows largely in one direction – downwards like a waterfall. For this reason, the waterfall model has been criticized as being unsuitable for dealing with unstable requirements in the software industry. Other criticisms as postulated by Alshamrani and Bahattab (2015), Kramer (2018) and Duggan (2006) include the following.

- All requirements must be known upfront. It cannot adopt major changes in requirements in the middle of the project.
- It must be inflexible.
- No working software is produced until late during the life cycle.

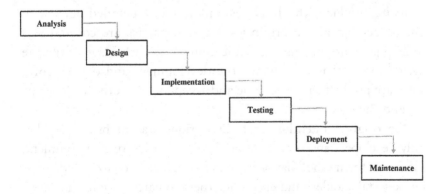

**Figure 1.4** The waterfall model.

- High amounts of risk and uncertainty. This increases with the expected time for the development of the project.
- User input is mostly garnered at the beginning of the project and not throughout the project cycle.
- Customers may have little opportunity to preview the software product until it may be too late.
- It is not preferred for complex projects.

### User-Centred Method

Born in 1974, the user-centred method was created to address the issue of limited user input and create an environment to guarantee that all uncertainties and miscommunication between the developer and the user are identified.

Joint Application Development (JAD) is one of the most popular user-centred methods (Wood & Silver, 1995) and is selected in this book not only for its popularity but for its benefits over the years. In a recent study using the JAD method, user satisfaction with the delivered software was as high as 84% (Sensuse et al., 2020).

The JAD software development method seeks to enhance user participation by involving the client or end user in the design and development of an application, through a succession of collaborative workshops called JAD sessions. The workshops consist of sessions where users/super users and developers meet to define and review the business requirements for the system. These JAD sessions sometimes take days in which the super users and the developers try to resolve any difficulties or differences regarding the new software product. The JAD sessions follow a detailed agenda to guarantee that all uncertainties between parties are covered and to help prevent any miscommunications at an early stage of the life cycle. The goal is to enhance the development and delivery of a software product that is feasible and acceptable to both the developers and the users.

The original intention of JAD sessions was to bring together only developers and users in a productive and creative environment. However, the method has become more sophisticated to include various key stakeholders and encourage them to participate in the development and delivery of the software product. These stakeholders are executive sponsors, subject matter experts, facilitator/session leaders, scribe/documentation experts, and observers, each playing different roles in the JAD sessions. The key steps are to:

1. identify project objectives and limitations;
2. identify critical success factors;
3. define project deliverables;
4. define the schedule of workshop activities;
5. select the participants;
6. organize workshop activities and exercises;
7. prepare, inform and educate the workshop participants; and
8. coordinate workshop logistics.

Duggan (2006) and Sensuse et al. (2020) have listed the following as advantages and disadvantages of the JAD method. Advantages include the decrease in time and costs relating to requirements management and bringing experts together, thus allowing the sharing of views and promoting a sense of project ownership. Additionally, technological applications like CASE tools can be integrated quite easily in the JAD sessions and the process can be replicated very easily. Despite the many advantages, users of the JAD should note that if detailed and thorough planning is not executed within JAD sessions, then valuable time can be easily wasted. Careful attention must be given to the selection of participants to ensure that those included can add value to the discussion. The facilitator must be capable of controlling the many problems that interacting groups can encounter (group think, destructive dominance, free loading and excessive socializing) to ensure that everyone has a chance to offer their opinions, ideas and thoughts.

### Reuse-Based Method

The reuse-based method was popularized in 1968 and was created to enhance cost savings and quality along the development cycle. It is a strategy in which the development process is geared towards reusing existing source codes or existing software. The availability of reusable software has increased drastically due to the proliferation of open-source developments, which has expanded the pool of reusable codes making them more affordable (Milka, 2017). The reuse-based development trend has been a response to the demand for faster delivery of software products-to-market, lower software production and maintenance costs and increased software quality.

Component-based development (CBD) is a reuse-based method of defining, implementing and composing loosely coupled independent components into software products. CBD is an extension of object-oriented programming (OOP) that accentuates the design and development of computer-based systems with the help of reusable software components. With CBD, the focus shifts from software programming to software system composing.

CBD methods involve procedures for developing software products by choosing ideal off-the-shelf components and then assembling them using a well-defined software architecture. Components communicate with each other via interfaces. With the systematic reuse and refinement of components, CBD seeks to deliver high-quality software products.

A common Login system at a bank is an example of a component. The codes behind this Login system does all the relevant and necessary authentication to identify the customer, whether doing a withdrawal, deposit, enquiry or applying for a loan at Bank A. The same codes behind this Login system can be used with transactions at Bank B.

There are a few advantages and disadvantages of the reuse-based method as stated by Barreto et al. (2011) and Jasmine and Vasantha (2010). The following advantages have been noted:

1. reduced development effort and cost;
2. accelerated software delivery;
3. increased likelihood of delivering high quality software products;
4. sound software engineering design principles; and
5. the ability to reuse components.

The disadvantages are that:

1. it takes significant effort and awareness to write a software component that is effectively reusable;
2. component trustworthiness can be a challenge;
3. there is difficulty in establishing interface standards;

4. it is unclear who will certify the quality of components and who will maintain the component registers; and

5. there is a critical mass of inventoried components.

Although CBD methods can stand on their own, in recent development they have been coupled with the incremental/iterative methods. This strategy is in alignment with the 'Silver pellets' concept to gradually chip away at the 'monster' of the software crisis.

### Incremental/Iterative Methods

The incremental/iterative method was created in 2001 to provide quick-to-market software products, risk mitigation and enhanced quality. Rapid application development (RAD) belongs to the incremental/iterative method. Unlike the waterfall method, it emphasizes early working software and user feedback over strict planning and requirements recording. In essence, it is less talk, more coding and frequent testing.

RAD was a response to the problems associated with the plan-driven waterfall method. Software can be used to radically change business processes and solve problems. Consequently, insights gained during the development process can be fed back to the requirements to assist in the design of business solutions. The plan-driven approaches attempt to rigidly define the requirements, the solution and the plan to implement it, and have a process that discourages changes. On the other hand, RAD approaches recognize that software development is a complex, knowledge-intensive process and provide flexible processes that help take advantage of insights gained during the project to improve business solutions. In addition, RAD facilitates the rapid development of prototypes, which can be tested for defects and functionality, as shown in Figure 1.5.

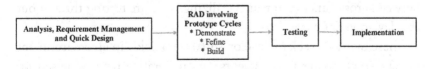

**Figure 1.5**  Rapid application development.

The advantages and disadvantages of RAD, as stated by Agarwal et al. (2000) and Berger and Beynon-Davies (2009), are as follows. Advantages include its applicability in a wide organizational context; the likelihood of a higher quality software product being developed and delivered in comparison to the waterfall model; better risk management based on early detection of defects in prototypes; and increased project success rate by focusing on the development of incremental modules. The disadvantages are its claim to be more suited for developing software that has a small to medium-sized project team; the likelihood of resistance to change by project members as some humans might be averse to change; the requirement of continual interaction throughout the entire project life-cycle between users and developers (such human resource might be scarce); and its focus on prototypes the testing of which can be costly.

### Agile Methods

Another method that belongs to the incremental/iterative method is the popular agile software development method (Lindskog & Magnusson, 2021). Agile software development is an umbrella term for a set of methods and practices based on the values and principles expressed in the Agile Manifesto. The incremental approach emphasizes people as the main determinants of software quality instead of process maturity. The agile development methods shun rigorous process structures while minimizing hindrances to expeditious software development by using an evolutionary strategy to quickly produce useful pieces of software functionality of high business value (Highsmith & Cockburn, 2001). The Agile Manifesto emphasizes incremental delivery, team collaboration (developers and users), continual planning, and continual learning and continual testing along the software development life cycle, instead of conducting the testing at the end of the development cycle (Highsmith & Cockburn, 2001). In other words, software products emerge through continual collaboration between cross-functional teams utilizing software testing throughout the development cycle.

These methods seek to develop software quickly in an environment of rapidly changing requirements, in an iterative manner based on the values and principles of the Agile Manifesto, with the ultimate goal of delivering high-quality software products that provide value to customers (Balijepally et al., 2009). Some of the principles employed in agile methods are:

- pair programming (two developers coding side by side);
- small and frequent releases of software;
- time-boxing;
- rigorous code testing; and
- frequent consultation with users (co-located teams with developers and users).

### Software Development Paradigms

After several years of software development challenges, two generic paradigms have emerged regarding the software planning continuum as shown in Figure 1.6. The extreme paradigms are milestone plan-driven and incremental software development. The plan-driven paradigm is popularly called structured development methods or process-centric, while the incremental development paradigm is more people-centric. Detractors from the structured paradigm claim that such rigid process structures impose large penalties in time and make the development process too cumbersome and disruptive (Boehm, 2002; Highsmith & Cockburn, 2001).

As stated earlier, software development is a complex activity with different views among key stakeholders regarding the determinants of project success (Barrett & Oborn, 2010). Studies have shown that many software development projects fail due to people problems (Ceschi et al., 2005; Qamar & Malik, 2020; Tam et al., 2020), with issues relating to communication at its centre. Communication problems between developers and users are the main reasons for conflicts (Boehm, 2002). At times there are different views regarding coding, user interface, screen navigation and security protocol.

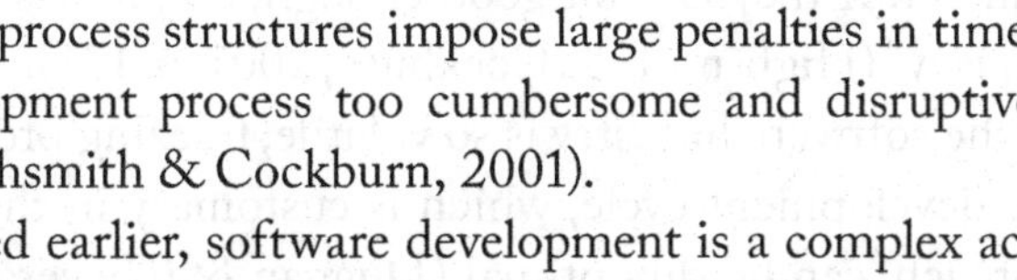

| Milestone Plan-Driven Method | Hybrid Method | Incremental Software Development |
|---|---|---|
| Waterfall Model | | Agile Methods |

**Figure 1.6**  The software planning continuum.

Though people problems can be a major reason for software project failure, it is suggested that factors such as executive management support, user involvement and emotional maturity skills are three ingredients required to ensure the successful execution of software projects. Emotional maturity skills include managing expectations and gaining consensus, which are people management competences. In their assessment the Standish Group (2015) recommends a 15% investment in efforts to boost emotional maturity, to realize greater improvement in project success.

Given the amount of emphasis being placed on people management, agile software development methods were introduced to resolve the communication problems that existed in software development. These agile methods rely on people's emotional maturity and creativity during software development rather than on the process maturity of firms (Nerur et al., 2005). In these agile methods users are actively shaping and guiding the incremental development and delivery of the software product along with developers (Dingsoyr et al., 2012). Proponents of this people view state that "if the people on the project are good enough, they can use almost any process and accomplish their assignment. If they are not good enough, no process will repair their inadequacy" (Highsmith & Cockburn, 2001, p. 131).

Because the software industry is so volatile, freezing project scope early in the development cycle, which is customary in the process-centric approach, can be suboptimal (Duggan & Chevers, 2008). It is considered suboptimal because users usually change their minds about what they want and need during the development cycle (commonly called requirements volatility). Along with unpredictable challenges, there is the need for speed-to-market which requires a shorter product life-cycle which is incompatible with plan-driven methods. The statistics in Table 1.3 outlines the success rates of the waterfall (plan-driven) versus agile methods (Standish Group, 2015).

The results of a study of more than 10,000 software projects between 2011 and 2015 show that agile projects have almost four times the success rate in comparison to waterfall projects, and waterfall projects have three times the failure rate as agile projects. It was also found that the smaller the project, the smaller the difference between agile and waterfall project success rates. Furthermore, it was discovered

**Table 1.3** Performance by Agile versus Waterfall Methods (2011–2015)

| SIZE | METHOD | SUCCESSFUL (%) | CHALLENGED (%) | FAILED (%) |
|---|---|---|---|---|
| All Size Projects | Agile | 39 | 52 | 9 |
| | Waterfall | 11 | 60 | 29 |
| Large Size Projects | Agile | 18 | 59 | 23 |
| | Waterfall | 3 | 55 | 42 |
| Medium Size Projects | Agile | 27 | 62 | 11 |
| | Waterfall | 7 | 68 | 25 |
| Small Size Projects | Agile | 58 | 38 | 4 |
| | Waterfall | 44 | 45 | 11 |

*Source:* Standish Group (2015).

that there are two 'trump cards' that, together, create a winning combination. These are agile methods coupled with small projects. The study found that small projects using an agile process only approach have a 4% failure rate.

Over time, the agile methods have been gaining in popularity (Lindskog & Magnusson, 2021). These methods include Scrum, Extreme programming (XP), Feature-driven development, Adaptive software, Crystal family of methods and Dynamic software development methods and Lean software development (Dyba & Dingsoyr, 2008). Studies have found that agile methods are being used in 65% of software projects (Ambler, 2006), with the scrum method currently being the most popular (Periyasamy & Chianelli, 2021; Sudha et al., 2021).

The advantages and disadvantages of agile methods, as stated by Oz (2009) and Tam et al. (2020), are that they seek to satisfy customers at the time of delivery, not at project initiation. A further advantage is that freezing project scope early is suboptimal because developers need to accommodate inevitable changes throughout the software development life cycle. It seeks to stabilize software quality, particularly in environments of high business process volatility and where systems requirements cannot be predetermined. The disadvantages of the agile methods are its underlying assumptions that the development team is both highly skilled and talented, and effectively managed by a competent and experienced project leader. This assumption can be flawed. In addition, agile methods could cause developers to deliver software ahead of business process changes or individuals' taste and preferences. This speed of delivery might only postpone the problem to the latter stage of the development life-cycle like support. This may aggravate another age-old software problem of maintainability. The lack of focus on architecture in agile methods can also create sub-optimal design-decisions. In addition, it is stated that agile methods are suitable for small teams working on small projects in pursuit of solving unstructured problems in cases where it is difficult for users to specify system requirements. Finally, agile methods are considered unsuitable for life-critical systems.

Studies have found that although agile methods, like scrum, are gaining in popularity, the traditional waterfall model is still being utilized. Interestingly, some organizations are taking a hybrid approach, using multiple methods on projects based on various contexts like project size, team characteristics and complexity (Vijayasarathy & Butler, 2016).

Nevertheless, in an effort to achieve both stability and responsiveness, many firms are embracing the combination of incremental and plan-driven approaches during the software development cycle (Dalton, 2016). Recently, firms that adopt the plan-driven approach, like the Capability Maturity Model Integration (CMMI), are utilizing agile methods, and likewise, firms that adopt the incremental approach (like agile) are utilizing the CMMI plan-driven approach to software development. It is said that the plan-driven approach provides a road map of 'what' must be done, whereas the agile approach prescribes 'how' it must be done (Dalton, 2016). This new trend of combining the plan-driven and incremental approaches has been reaping various benefits and successes.

Minacs IT Services, an outsourcing company with headquarters in the US, Canada and India, that embraced both plan-driven and incremental methods experienced a 30–40% increase in attaining an agile technique called sprint, a 30% increase in the number of user stories delivered in each sprint and a 40% increase in on-time-delivery. Similarly, a global high technology company – Perficient Chennai – was able to reduce software defects by 70% by adopting both plan-driven and incremental methods (Dalton, 2016). Consequently, the integration of both methods is a growing trend.

Based on these findings, it is recommended that a disciplined and multi-method attack be employed to overcome the problem of delivering poor quality software products. A silver pellet approach should be taken to assess the effectiveness of various methods and/ or the combination of various methods in respective contexts. It should be noted that these methods do not present a major divide in developed versus developing economies but if adapted appropriately can offer an opportunity to deliver high-quality software products. However, special care should be taken by way of testing and quality assurance to ensure the attainment of critical quality attributes.

Although great strides have been made through the evolution of the production methods, it is strongly believed that the main determinants of software quality are people, process and technology: people being the champion of the project and the guardian of the delivered software product, the developmental process being documented and institutionalized, and the adaptation of the right technology to achieve a defect-free software product.

## References

Agarwal, R., Prasad, J., Tanniru, M., & Lynch, J. (2000). Risks of rapid application development. *Communications of ACM*, *43*(11), 177–189.

Al Obisat, F. M., Alhalhouli, Z. T., Aleawashdel, T. I., & Alshaabatat, T. E. (2018). Review of literature on software quality. *World of Computer Science and Information Technology Journal*, *8*(5), 32–42.

Alshamrani, A., & Bahattab, A. (2015). A comparison between three SDLC models waterfall model, spiral model, and incremental/iterative model. *International Journal of Computer Science Issues*, *12*(1), 106–111.

Ambler, S. (2006). Agile adoption rate survey. Retrieved from http://www. serena.com/docs/repository/solutions/intro-to-agile-devel.pdf. Accessed on January 3, 2017.

Anees, A., & Agrwal, A. (2017). Software process improvement models and their comparison. *International Journal of Advanced Research in Computer Science*, *8*(5), 928–932.

Balijepally, V., Mahapatra, R., Nerur, S., & Price, K. (2009). Are two heads better than one for software development? The productivity paradox of pair programming. *MIS Quarterly*, *33*(1), 91–118.

Barreto, A. S., Murta, L. G. P., & Da Rocha, A. R. (2011). Software process definition: A reuse-based approach. *Journal of Universal Computer Science*, *17*(13), 1765–1799.

Barrett, M., & Oborn, E. (2010). Boundary object use in cross-cultural software development teams. *Human Relations*, *63*(8), 1199–1221.

Berger, H., & Beynon-Davies, P. (2009). The utility of rapid application development in large-scale, complex projects. *Information Systems Journal*, *19*, 549–570.

Boehm, B. (2002). Get ready for agile methods, with care. *IEEE Computer*, *35*(1), 64–69.

Brooks, F. (1987). No silver bullet: Essence and accidents of software engineering. *Computer Magazine*, 1–13. Retrieved from http://virtualschool.edu/mon/SoftwareEngineering/BrooksNoSilverBullet.html. Accessed on July 26, 2017.

Brynjolfsson, E. (1993). The productivity paradox of information technology. *Communications of the ACM*, *36*(12), 67–77.

Carrozza, G., Pietrantuono, R., & Russo, S. (2018). A software quality framework for large-scale mission-critical systems engineering. *Information and Software Technology*, *102*, 100–116.

Ceschi, M., Sillitti, A., & Succi, G. (2005). Project management in plan-based and agile companies. *IEEE Software*, *22*(3), 21–27.

Chevers, D. A., Mills, A. M., Duggan, E., & Moore, S. (2020). A software process improvement model for small firms in developing countries. In Zuopeng (Justin) Zhang (Ed.), *Novel theories and applications of global information resource management* (pp. 47–80). Pennsylvania: IGI Global.

Dalton, J. (2016). A guide to Scrum and CMMI: Improving agile performance with CMMI. *CMMI Institute*, 1–130.

Dingsoyr, T., Nerur, S., Balijepally, V., & Moe, N. (2012). A decade of agile methodologies: Towards explaining agile software development. *The Journal of System and Software*, *85*(6), 1213–1221.

Duggan, E. W. (2003). Silver pellets for improving software quality. *Information Resources Management Journal*, *17*(2), 1–21.

Duggan, E. W. (2006). Tranquilizing the werewolf that attacks information systems quality. In Mehdi Khosrow-Pour (Ed.), *Advanced topics in information resources management* (pp. 253–281). Pennsylvania: IGI Global.

Duggan, E. W., & Chevers, D. A. (2008). *Agile systems development versus process-centricity: A conflict of priorities?* Paper presented at the International Conference on Information Resources Management (Conf-IRM), Niagara Fall, Ontario, Canada.

Dwivedi, Y. K., Wastell, D., Laumer, S., Henriksen, H. Z., Myers, M. D., Bunker, D., Elbanna, A., Ravishankar, M. N., & Srivastava, S. C. (2014). Research on information systems failures and success: Status update and future directions. *Information System Frontier*, *17*(1), 143–157.

Dyba, T., & Dingsoyr, T. (2008). Empirical studies of agile software development: A systematic review. *Information and Software Technology*, *50*, 833–859.

Fitzpatrick, R. (1996). Software quality: Definitions and strategic issues. *Dublin Institute of Technology*, 1–35.

Gibbs, W. W. (1994). Software's chronic crisis. *Scientific American*, *271*(3), 86–95.

Gladden, G. R. (1982). Stop the life-cycle, I want to get off. *ACM SZGSOFT Software Engineering Notes*, *7*(2), 35–39.

Highsmith, J., & Cockburn, A. (2001). Agile software development: The business of innovation. *Software Management*, *34*(9), 120–122.

Hossain, M. D. S. (2018). Challenges of software quality assurance and testing. *International Journal of Software Engineering and Computer Systems, 4*(1), 133–144.

ISO. (1991). *ISO/IEC 9126: Information technology - Software product evaluation - Quality characteristics and guidelines for their use.* International Standard Organization.

Jasmine, K. S., & Vasantha, R. (2010). A new capability maturity model for reuse based software development process. *International Journal of Engineering and Technology, 2*(1), 112–123.

Joslin, R., & Muller, R. (2016). The impact of project methodologies on project success in different project environments. *International Journal of Managing Projects in Business, 9*(2), 364–388.

Kabore, S. E., Sane, S., & Abo, P. (2021). Transformational leadership and success of international development projects (ID projects): Moderating role of the project team size. *Leadership and Organization Development Journal, 42*(4), 517–530.

Kittlaus, H. B., & Clough, P. N. (2009). Software products: Terms and characteristics. In *Software product management and pricing* (pp. 5–18). Berlin Heideberg: Springer.

Kramer, M. (2018). Best practices in systems development lifecycle: An analysis based on the waterfall model. *Review of Business & Finance Studies, 9*(1), 77–84.

Krasner, H. (2021). The cost of poor software quality in the US: A 2020 report. *Consortium for Information and Software Quality*, 1–46.

Laudon, K. C., & Laudon, J. P. (2015). *Management information systems: Managing the digital firms* (14th ed.). Upper Saddle River, NJ: Pearson Prentice Hall.

Lindskog, C., & Magnusson, M. (2021). Ambidexterity in agile software development: A conceptual paper. *Journal of Organizational Effectiveness: People and Performance, 8*(1), 16–43.

Milka, I. (2017). Reuse of software engineering. *International Scientific Journal*, 1–4.

Nerur, S. R., Mahapatra, R., & Mangalaraj, G. (2005). Challenges of migrating to agile methodologies. *Communications of ACM, 48*(5), 73–78.

Oz, E. (2009). *Management information systems* (6th ed.). Boston, MA: Thomson.

Periyasamy, K., & Chianelli, J. (2021). A project tracking tool for scrum projects with machine learning support for cost estimation. *EPiC Series in Computing, 76*, 86–94.

Perlroth, N. (2019). Apple was slow to act on FaceTime bug that allows spying on iPhones. *New York Times*, 1–8.

Porter, M. E., & Millar, V. E. (1985). How information gives you competitive advantage. *Harvard Business Review, 63*(4), 149–160.

Qamar, N., & Malik, A. A. (2020`). Determining the relative importance of personality traits in influencing software quality and team productivity. *Computing and Informatics, 39*, 994–1021.

Quintin, C. (2018). Our cellphones aren't safe. *New York Times*, 1–5.

Schulmeyer, G. G., & McManus, J. I. (1999). *The Handbook of software quality assurance* (3rd ed.). Upper Saddle River, NJ: Prentice Hall, Inc.

Sensuse, D. I., Riochman, H. N., Hakim, S., & Winarni, W. (2020). Knowledge management system design method with joint application design (JAD) adoption. *VINE Journal of Information and Knowledgement Systems, 51*(1), 27–46.

Sorensen, M. S. (2019). Flaws in cellphone evidence prompt review of 10,000 verdicts in Denmark. *New York Times*, 1–5.

Standish Group, T. (2015). Standish group 2015 Chaos report. *The Standish Group*, 1–16.

Sudha, N., Kumar, S. S., Rengarajan, A., & Rao, K. B. (2021). Scrum based scaling using agile method to test software projects using artificial neural networks for block chain. *Annals of Romanian Society for Cell Biology, 25*(4), 3711–3727.

Tam, C., Moura, E. J., Oliveira, T., & Varajao, J. (2020). The factors influencing the success of on-going agile software development projects. *International Journal of Project Management, 38*, 165–176.

Tassey, G. (2002). The economic impacts of inadequate infrastructure for software testing. *National Institute of Standards and Technology*, 1–309.

Vijayasarathy, L. R., & Butler, C. W. (2016). Choice of software development methodologies: Do organizational, project, and team characteristics matter? *IEEE Software, 33*(5), 86–94.

Wong, B. (2006). Different views of software quality. In E. W. Duggan & H. Reichgelt (Eds.), *Measuring information systems delivery quality* (pp. 55–84). Hershey: Idea Group.

Wood, J., & Silver, D. (1995). *Joint application development* (2nd ed.). New York: Wiley.

Zeineddine, R., & Mansour, N. (2005). SQIMSO: Quality improvement for small software organizations. *Journal of Computer Science, 1*(3), 316–322.

# 2

# The Strategic Use of Technology in Software Development

It is believed that the main determinants of software quality are people, process and technology (Ghayyur et al., 2018; Gorla & Lin, 2010; Knauer et al., 2020; Tam et al., 2020). However, this chapter will focus on the strategic use of technology in the software development life cycle. The cycle is used in software engineering to describe a process of planning, requirements management, software design, implementation, testing and evolution/maintenance in building software products. It is imperative that each stage of the cycle be completed with special care to avoid any kind of quality issues or software defects being delivered to the customer/user.

All craftsmen need tools in order to effectively execute their jobs. An auto mechanic needs an array of wrenches, sockets and impact tools. A carpenter needs an assortment of hammers, screwdrivers, chisels and measuring tapes. Likewise, the software developer needs the right software tools to effectively accomplish his/her assigned tasks along the development cycle. These tools can be classified as software development tools, automated testing tools and project management tools.

Project teams often undergo extensive planning processes before undertaking the implementation stage of a project. Getting all members of the project team to work as one is usually very difficult to achieve, but project management tools can enhance team building. The team building feature is very important because in today's environment most software projects function as distributed teams. That means that team members are in different locations physically (locally and overseas) and/or work for organizations which manage multiple projects simultaneously. In addition, in earlier days, project managers would use various tools for various functions. One tool to

DOI: 10.1201/9781003388944-2

communicate with team members, another for task management, another for file sharing and another for reporting. Using a project management tool provides a holistic way to effectively and efficiently manage a project. It has been reported, also, that 9.9% of every dollar invested in a project is wasted due to poor project planning, allocation and utilization of resources (Langley, 2019). If your project is running over budget, take a close look at how tasks are scheduled, the sequencing of the tasks and the utilization of all resources (human and physical). Hence, the main purpose of project management tools is to assist project managers to plan, execute, monitor and control all stages of the project. Ultimately, conforming to the 'iron triangle' of delivering the project within time, within budget and with the stated quality specifications.

On the other hand, software development tools are a set of computer programs that are used by software developers to create, maintain and debug software products. These tools can function as an interpreter that works directly with the source code, but they can also be tools that help to make the work of a software developer simpler and easier. The selection of software development tools used in the development cycle can shape or break a project. Similarly, automated testing is the application of software tools to automate a human-driven manual process of reviewing and validating a software product. Automated tests can be conducted much faster than manual tests, and seek to meet quality, safety, security and privacy requirements before the software product is released into production and ultimately delivered to the customer. Machines will process data faster and are more mobile and more flexible. As a result, automated tests reduce testing efforts, provide faster delivery of software products and facilitate more affordable products. These are the central tenets of automated testing which can, ultimately, lead to sustained competitive advantage.

### Project Management Tools

There are several tools which can be leveraged at various stages of the software development cycle as shown in Table 2.1. This chapter will first explore project management tools followed by software development tools and finally automated testing tools. These tools work together to deliver high-quality software products and successful projects.

**Table 2.1**    Software Development Life Cycle Tools

| NO. | SOFTWARE DEVELOPMENT LIFE CYCLE | SOFTWARE DEVELOPMENT TOOL | SOFTWARE LICENSE |
|---|---|---|---|
| **PROJECT MANAGEMENT** | | | |
| 1 | Project Management (Overarching and necessary for the entirety of projects) | Microsoft Project | Proprietary |
| | | Primavera Project Planner | Proprietary |
| | | ShotGrid | Proprietary |
| | | Jira | Free + Pay plans |
| | | Trello | Free + Pay plans |
| | | TeamGantt | Free + Pay plans |
| | | Teamwork Project | Free + Pay plans |
| | | Zoho Project | Free + Pay plans |
| **SOFTWARE DEVELOPMENT** | | | |
| 2 | Requirements Gathering | ReqSuite | Free trial + Pay plans |
| | | MindManager | Free trial + Pay plans |
| | | Accompa | Free trial + Pay plans |
| 3 | Software Design | Autodesk Product Design Suite | Proprietary |
| | | RAD Studio | Free trial + Pay plans |
| | | MechDesigner | Free trial + Pay plans |
| 4 | Code Generation | Reegenerator | Proprietary |
| | | Bitbucket | Free + Pay plans |
| | | Json2Kotlin | Free (FOSS) |
| 5 | Collaborate (Implementation with Distributed Teams) | Confluence | Free + Pay plans |
| | | GitHub | Free + Pay plans |
| | | Google Workspace | Free trial + Pay plans |
| | | Microsoft Teams | Free + Pay plans |
| 6 | Software Testing | ALM/Quality Centre | Proprietary |
| | | Selenium | Free + Pay plans |
| | | Apache JMeter | Free (FOSS) |

As stated earlier, project management tools are used to plan, organize, define tasks and responsibilities, keep track of the project's progress and allocate resources for the successful execution of the project. These tools allow the project manager to better control costs and time and allow for smooth collaboration among key stakeholders. Collaboration features are especially important when projects utilize distributed teams.

Project management tools such as Microsoft Project, Primavera, JIRA, Teamwork Project, Trello and others facilitate the planning and management of software projects from conception to evolution/ maintenance, and ensure that tasks and processes are well defined, organized, documented and transparent. Software development tools, on the other hand, deal with the actual development of the software and utilize various tools through the different stages of the software development life cycle as shown in Table 2.1. Although many of these tools are proprietary software, some can be accessed as free and open-source software (FOSS), while others have free trials with subsequent payment plans.

Proprietary software, also known as non-free software or closed-source software, is computer software for which the software developer reserves some rights from licences to use, modify, share modifications or share the software. In contrast, free and open-source software (FOSS) is a broad term used to describe software developed and released under an open-source licence allowing inspection, modification and redistribution of the software's source without charge (Crowston et al., 2007).

Microsoft Project by Microsoft and Primavera Project Planner by Oracle are some examples of proprietary software products. The cloud-based solutions of Microsoft Project payment plans range from US$10 to US$55 per user per month, whereas a typical 'free' project management software such as Trello and TeamGantt can range from US$0 to US$79 per month for 50 users. It is felt that many small software development firms in developing economies might not be able to acquire the proprietary development tools due to financial, human and physical constraints. However, these small firms can avoid being caught off-guard by unwanted software errors due to a lack of resources because they can adapt the free and open-source tools.

Both proprietary and FOSS project management tools have similar features which can enhance the performance of projects, with respect to the timing and budgetary aspects of the 'iron triangle'. However, storage capacity is a major differentiator between free and proprietary software tools, with free software, typically, offering in the range of 100 MB of storage while proprietary counterparts, typically, offer unlimited storage. Although free, some FOSS applications could rival fee-based applications in terms of benefits and features. However, some software developers and users might perceive that FOSS applications do not have adequate features and functionalities to satisfy their needs. It is also important to note that there usually is uncertainty regarding after-sale service and maintenance of FOSS applications.

Notwithstanding, Microsoft Project is the *de facto* standard for project management. The popularity of Microsoft Project is in alignment with a survey that was conducted in Jamaica (a developing economy) in January 2022 among 75 developers. In the study, it was discovered that Microsoft Project (a proprietary tool) was the dominant tool used in project management, but other tools with free payment options like Trello and Teamwork Project were also utilized. The same study also found that Apache JMeter (a free and open-source software) was being used as a software testing tool in Jamaica. This finding confirms the trend that various tools (project management and software development tools) are utilized at different stages of the software development cycle.

### Stages of Project Management

The desire to satisfy customers starts from the conception/idea generation (the first stage of the project management cycle) of the project. The additional stages comprise planning, executing, controlling and terminating. The following are applicable examples of using project management tools to increase the likelihood of delivering software projects within budget and on time.

1. Concept or idea generation

    Most project management tools have a collaboration facility and/or online Kanban facility. These facilities enhance idea generation among the project sponsor, project managers, developers and users. Group discussion techniques such as mind maps, brainstorming, reverse thinking and story boarding are employed in many of these sessions. The employment of these techniques can suppress various group interacting problems like group think, destructive dominance, free loading and excessive socializing. Consequently, the benefit of using these facilities and techniques is the likelihood of designing the best solution within a reasonable time.

2. Planning

    It is easy to create a project plan with the aid of a project management tool. In addition, the exercise of establishing a dependent relationship among the tasks, prioritizing the tasks, allocating resources, setting up deadlines and creating deliverables is easily done within a reasonable time when compared to manual execution. Project management tools help to streamline the project planning and scheduling process.

Most of these tools use the Gantt chart as the baseline for the planning of the project and utilize the principle of program evaluation review technique (PERT) for the management of projects. PERT takes a scientific approach to project management and assists the project manager with timely responses to important questions such as:

(i) When will the entire project be completed?

(ii) What are the critical activities in the project?

(iii) Which are the non-critical activities?

(iv) What is the probability that the project will be completed by a specific date?

(v) At any date, is the project on schedule, behind schedule or ahead of schedule?

(vi) On a given date, is the money spent equal to, less than or greater than the budgeted amount?

(vii) Are there enough resources available to finish the project on time?

These are critical questions that can be answered with the click of a button, thus making the project manager more productive, efficient and effective. In addition, most project management tools do an excellent job with respect to document management. It is also important to note that the record of a previously similar project can be accessed easily by the relevant project personnel.

3. Executing

The project tracking facility of most project management tools allows all data, information and communication on the project to be in one central repository, which makes it easy to assign tasks and define priorities. The current project management trend is to keep every detail of a project centralized in real time so that up-to-date information can flow freely among people, and across processes and tools. Project managers can easily delegate tasks to members and find who is available at that moment. It is also easy to keep track of team members' work, as well as the progress of other projects (multiple projects at the same time).

The performance of actual versus planned activities can be easily measured and reported. Some project management tools utilize the concept of scrum boards and agile reporting facilities to track the progress of the project and report the performance of the project.

A scrum board is a visual way of managing and organizing projects and breaking down activities into different stages of completion. Some stages are to do, doing, reviewing and completed. On the other hand, agile reporting is a technique which analyses and shares information about a project using specific software and methods of reporting. There are two categories of agile reports. One is designed for personnel external to the project and the other is designed for personnel internal to the project. The information in each report is different but serves the purpose of aiding informed decision-making.

Accessing and sharing important reports/documents is very important and common in the execution of projects. Provisions are in place for users to make changes, log their feedback, track software errors (bugs), view outstanding issues and monitor the execution of tasks. These features can facilitate the on-time completion of the project within budget.

4. Controlling

During any project, the possibility exists for scope creep, which is the tendency of the project to go off track. Software projects are noted for experiencing scope creep. Most project management tools can assist project managers by allowing them to keep track of all activities and resources on a real-time and online basis. This feature, by extension, can prevent the project cost from going over budget.

It is important to note that the team members of recent projects are usually recruited from different countries or from different areas across an organization (called distributed teams). The gap in distance and time zone differences can make it a challenge for all key project personnel to attend meetings regularly and be kept updated. This communication gap can create unnecessary delays in the completion of the project. However, most project management tools have a collaboration facility which can bridge this communication gap.

Based on the volume of data in the one central repository, the project manager is better able to identify and manage all possible risks. In general, it is important to note that the benefits of using project management tools as stated by Ambler (2001), Saratkar (2019) and Wilson (2007) are:

  (i) improved planning and scheduling;
  (ii) better collaboration among all key stakeholders working remotely;
  (iii) improved productivity of developers/project managers;
  (iv) effective task delegation, greater control of resources;
  (v) easier file access and sharing; improved tracking of project's performance;
  (vi) easier integration of new members, improved communication;
  (vii) effective risk mitigation; and
  (viii) improved budget management.

5. Terminating

In earlier days, it was imperative for the project sponsor, project manager, team members and users to conduct a physical walk through of the delivered software product before the closure of the project was authorized. There is now no need for the physical presence of key personnel. Instead, computer simulation can be performed on the delivered software product and informed decisions made regarding the authorization of payment and the closure of the project. Several activities are being done virtually which saves on time and cost.

Based on the examples cited earlier, the benefits of project management tools and techniques are shared documents, calendars and contacts. These are very important features in cases where projects are outsourced. It is much easier to perform tasks without having to send hundreds of emails with attached documents, which can lead to missing documents and misunderstanding. Project team members can collaborate on a variety of project tasks. In addition, having access to the calendars of all project members facilitates more efficient coordination of activities.

With project management tools, seamless collaboration can be accomplished. Team members can quickly contact the right person and get immediate guidance whenever the need for clarity arises. Further, these tools enable file sharing, documentation and detailed reporting. In addition, project management tools allow project managers to optimize cost and to maximize profits via time tracking, progress monitoring and tracking, and budget reporting and, thus, only purchase needed resources. It is customary for members of a distributed project team to prepare different information from different tasks. Consequently, it is critical to make respective information available and accessible to all members of the team for transparent and effective communication.

Another salient point is the fact that most project managers would like to see the 'big picture' of the project and the project schedule can satisfy that desire. Project management tools can optimize the project's workflow, enhance the software developer's productivity, and reduce development time, which, by extension, can increase profits.

Finally, one important benefit of most project management tools is the cloud-based service that they provide. Again, this utility (cloud-based technology) is important as project teams are becoming larger and more remote, so better collaboration can be accommodated with this technology. The cloud-based approach is believed to be more economical than buying a licence for the software. This approach facilitates flexibility and scalability and is available to both large and small firms, whether in developed or developing economies.

In general, project managers and software developers are merging project management tools and techniques and software development tools, in an effort to overcome the software crisis. The ultimate goal is to develop software products that take less time to market, improve efficiency and productivity, reduce cost and improve quality (Saratkar, 2019). These tools and techniques are being utilized at various stages along the software development life cycle to balance the budget, time and quality of the delivered software products.

As shown in Table 2.1, while Microsoft Project, for example, is being used by the project manager as the overarching tool to manage the entire project, the software developer might be using 'ReqSuite' for requirements gathering, 'MechDesigner' for software design, 'Reegenerator' for code generation, 'Confluence' for collaboration and 'Selenium' for software testing.

However, there can be an excellent project manager with a very good team of software developers who utilize the best tools at the appropriate time but without frequent and robust testing the probability of delivering high-quality software products might be low (Hossain, 2018). Consequently, the project team needs to seek the support of software testing in the development cycle.

### Automated Testing Tools

In an attempt to increase the likelihood of delivering high-quality software products without software defects, it is imperative that adequate and relevant testing be done (Narayan, 2018). The current trend regarding software testing is the utilization of automated testing tools. The potential benefits of software development automation include a reduction of the development cycle time and an improvement in the quality of the software product delivered due to the unravelling of various inconsistencies, duplications and defects (errors) during development. As a result, software defects do not have to be 'the evil in the dark anymore' because of the wide range of software development tools on the market that can provide visibility into the 'darkness'.

Software testing teams can leverage artificial intelligence (AI) and machine learning (ML) to improve their automation strategies, as well as ensure software security which is a critical property that cannot be overlooked during software development (Mikhalchuk, 2020). Automated testing can increase the overall test scope which, by extension, can improve software quality (Narayan, 2018). AI and ML algorithms are being used to improve the performance of the 'iron triangle' measures, as well as improve the performance along the software development life cycle (from requirement gathering to software testing) as shown in Table 2.2. The utilization of AI and ML in software testing can improve users' experience (Maloney, 2020).

Consequently, AI and ML are currently being viewed as the main technological tools to support software testing. They enable fast, accurate and continuous testing that improves the developmental process to the extent that bugs/errors are identified and fixed before the software product is released. This shortens the developmental process, as well as increases the delivery of high-quality software products. AI and ML in tandem can automatically detect, diagnose and repair

**Table 2.2** Comparing the Characteristics of Software Development Tools

| SOFTWARE DEVELOPMENT TOOLS | | ARTIFICIAL INTELLIGENCE | MACHINE LEARNING | PROJECT MANAGEMENT | REQSUITE | MECH DESIGNER | CONFLUENCE | SELENIUM |
|---|---|---|---|---|---|---|---|---|
| Iron Triangle | Quality | ✓ | ✓ | | | | | |
| | Time | | | ✓ | | | | |
| | Budget | | | ✓ | | | | |
| Software Development Life Cycle | Requirements Gathering | ✓ | ✓ | ✓ | ✓ | | ✓ | |
| | Software Design | ✓ | ✓ | ✓ | | ✓ | | |
| | Implementation | | | ✓ | | | | |
| | Testing | ✓ | ✓ | | | | | ✓ |
| | Evolution | | | | | | | |

software errors without developer intervention. This drives the developmental costs down and improves efficiency. In addition, AI and ML algorithms go further to predict and prevent software errors by automatically searching through databases and series of codes to uncover abnormalities and outliers and prescribe an array of recommendations which can help developers avoid similar errors in the future (Narayan, 2018). It is for these reasons that AI is seen as the 'co-pilot' to the developer. Interestingly, a growing number of AI-based tools to support software development are being made available for free (Schatsky & Bumb, 2020), thereby minimizing the digital divide between large and small software development firms.

Artificial intelligence is defined as machines that mimic human intelligence in tasks such as learning, planning and problem-solving through higher-level autonomous knowledge creation (De Bruyn et al., 2020). Machine learning (ML) is an important enablement aspect of AI. ML can predict and effectively schedule resources based on massive data inputs (Zhao et al., 2019). In ML, the algorithms analyse large volumes of data to learn patterns and relationships so that it is able to predict outcomes. As more data is entered into these models, the models become more accurate at making predictions. This results in ML becoming very useful in automating various elements of software development.

Both AI and ML are applicable in various stages of the software development life cycle. These stages include requirements gathering, automated project budgeting and estimating, software design, automated code generation, software testing, strategic decision-making and deployment. The following are applicable examples of using AI and ML to increase the likelihood of delivering high-quality software products.

1. Requirements Gathering

   Requirements gathering utilizes a vast amount of human interaction because it seeks to identify what the user needs from the proposed software product. As a result, the aim of these AI tools like Google ML Kit and Infosys Nia is to automate certain procedures in the requirements management stage, in an effort to minimize human interactions. These tools are powered by a technique called natural language processing which can analyse requirements documents, detect inconsistencies, flag ambiguities, identify incomplete requirements, observe compound requirements and subsequently suggest improvement opportunities. These tools not only improve the quality of the software product, but they also reduce requirements gathering time.

2. Software Design

There is always the search for unique and creative designs relating to software products. Hence, developers need specialized knowledge, learning and experience to propose the best software solution. Settling on the most appropriate and best software design (solution) is an error-prone task for developers. To reach the appropriate solution, the developer must have a visionary solution and be able to express the solution in physical terms.

AI tools such as artificial intelligence design assistant (AIDA) can be used to automate some difficult tasks. AIDA is a website-building platform that examines various combinations of software designs and presents the appropriate customized solution based on the user's needs, thus increasing the quality of the software product.

3. Automated Code Generation

Being confronted with a business problem and writing codes to resolve the issue is time-consuming and labour intensive. In an effort to simplify the process, automated code generation is being utilized in many software development firms. Artificial intelligence tools like Tara, Kite and Deep TabNine are being used by developers to gain new knowledge, streamline processes, and improve the speed and accuracy during the coding process. In essence, the goal is to write simple, clean and better codes. The introduction of these tools allows developers to dedicate more time to problem-solving and creating more creative software solutions.

4. Software Testing

Efficient testing is crucial to ensure optimum software product quality (Hossain, 2018). Testing can also be a time-consuming, costly and manual task with a high margin of error. Software errors can easily slip through the cracks and only be detected after the product has been released. Artificial intelligence tools like Appvance, Functionize and Testim are a few examples of

AI and machine-based testing platforms. These tools find errors and fix the bugs in the code before the product is released, thus ensuring shortened development time and higher-quality software products being delivered. In addition, AI helps developers in the formulation of use cases. This formulation is achieved by collecting data from the system logs and providing automated test cases.

The following are applicable examples of using AI and ML to assist in measuring a project's completion time and budget.

1. Automated Project Budgeting and Estimating

   A large majority of projects are not delivered on time and within budget as software development estimates (both time and cost) are always challenging. Software development is complex and so it is difficult to accurately predict the obstacles that might be encountered along the cycle and the severity of these obstacles. As a result, software development firms are using AI to improve the management of their projects. In general, these AI tools apply advanced data analytics with the requirements data, project scope, IT infrastructure and prior project data to automatically predict project budget and timelines. This can make project planning more accurate and project execution more efficient.

   An example is how Crane Ai uses AI-enabled project planning to create accurate estimates for delivering apps. As new requirements are entered the platform adjusts the project in real time. The platform can ingest code changes as they are entered and subsequently predict how these changes impact the project cost and time estimates.

2. Strategic Decision-Making

   Significant time is required in planning to transform requirements into a software product. In general, software development firms are exploring the possibilities of implementing several competing projects. As a result, there is always the need to prioritize projects as well as determine the ones to be eliminated or postponed. AI can be employed to explore the feasibility of competing projects.

   In addition, AI is revolutionizing the way businesses are conducted from data-based decision-making to autonomous operations. Consequently, AI needs to analyse vast amounts of data, with the view of providing critical insights in an effort to make informed decisions, not by human subjects but by AI itself. An example is found in the healthcare sector in which image recognition and analysis is an essential part of AI and ML. These technologies can be used for diagnostic purposes in the health-care sector with the goal of saving lives. Radiologists use CT scans for the diagnosis of cancer, but they have to review numerous scans every day. This is a time-consuming and tedious task, coupled with the fact that China is experiencing human resource constraints (a lack of radiologists) to go through billions of CT scans each year. Also, overworked healthcare professionals might suffer from fatigue which, in turn, can cause serious errors. Consequently, AI is being adopted to fill the gap to detect early signs of cancer. This development makes the radiologists' job much easier because they can use the analysis from the AI to diagnose and predict for cancer more accurately and efficiently. Another example is that a trained AI system in Germany is able to recognize skin cancer on photographs better than most doctors with average levels of experience.

3. Deployment Management

The deployment phase is the stage at which developers upgrade the software to the production environment. If developers fail to execute this process correctly during the upgrade, there can be a high risk of project failure. AI can prevent these vulnerabilities and increase the probability of delivering a successful project.

Automated software deployment is the auto-distribution of all modules in a working environment with zero to minimal manual intervention. Software deployment can be a daunting task for project managers and software developers because of the ever-growing number of endpoints. Lumen is a leading AI deployment software; it allows organizations to develop and deploy artificial intelligence into the cloud.

Artificial intelligence (AI) and machine learning (ML) are having a significant impact on the design and delivery of software products, especially as modern customers live on the 'always-on' mode and require everything to be at their fingertips and working properly.

It is said that AI and ML are helping to make better software products. Hence, it is imperative that software development firms understand the impact of AI and ML and their potential benefits not only in building software products but also in the quality dimensions (maintainability, reliability, functionality, usability, efficiency and portability) of the software product.

Prior studies have found that tools used in software development have had a positive impact on the quality of source code, the productivity of software developers and the quality of documentation (Bendure, 1991; Ravichandran & Rai, 2000; Rummens & Sucher, 1989; Williamson, 1990). In their study, Coupe and Onodu (1996) discovered that software development tools have a positive effect on software quality, especially the quality characteristics of reliability and functionality. Consistent delivery of these quality characteristics can lead to sustained competitive advantage.

Although software testing can be an expensive process, the adoption of these tools can be feasible in small firms, because the costs of these technologies are being reduced (Ernst, 2021). The reduction in the cost of digital technologies has significantly lowered barriers to entry for firms to enter the software industry (Ernst, 2021). In addition, these technologies are known to increase the productivity of developers. However, the implementation and adoption of the latest technology on its own may not necessarily improve the quality of the software being delivered. Key stakeholders in the development cycle must be properly trained and a clearly defined process roadmap understood.

Consequently, a coherent and integrated strategy encompassing all identified factors is required for quality software development. Technology by itself can be an enabler of better-quality software products and provide a medium for efficiency and productivity. However, the development cycle demands the balancing of technology, process and people for the most effective results. It is important to note that many technically sound software products with the requisite quality characteristics might not be used because they are perceived as not being useful or easy to use, or seen as a threat. Without usage, the expected benefits of individual's satisfaction or business value might not be realized.

# References

Ambler, S. W. (2001). When should you use CASE tools? Retrieved from http://www.ibm.com/developerworks/library/co-tipuse.html. Accessed on January 3, 2017.

Bendure, C. O. (1991). A case study on CASE: Its evolution and use at HHMI. *Journal of Information Systems Management, 8*(4), 50–56.

Coupe, R. T., & Onodu, N. M. (1996). An empirical evaluation of the impact of CASE on developer productivity and software quality. *Journal of Information Technology, 11,* 173–181.

Crowston, K., Li, Q., Wei, K., Eseryel, U. Y., & Howison, J. (2007). Self-organization of teams for free/libre open source software development. *Information and Software Technology, 49*(6), 564–575.

De Bruyn, A., Viswanathan, V., Beh, Y. S., Brook, J. K., & Wangenheim, F. (2020). Artificial intelligence and marketing: Pitfalls and opportunities. *Journal of Interactive Marketing, 51,* 91–105.

Ernst, E. (2021). The economics of artificial intelligence: An agenda by Ajay Agrawal, Joshua Gans and Avi Goldfarb. *Pluto Journals, 37*(2), 191–197.

Ghayyur, S. A. J., Ahmed, S., Ali, M., Razzaq, A., & Ahmed, N. (2018). A systematic literature review of success factors and barriers of agile software development. *International Journal of Advanced Computer Science and Applications, 9*(3), 278–289.

Gorla, N., & Lin, S. (2010). Determinants of software quality: A survey of information systems project managers. *Information and Software Technology, 52,* 602–610.

Hossain, M. D. S. (2018). Challenges of software quality assurance and testing. *International Journal of Software Engineering and Computer Systems, 4*(1), 133–144.

Knauer, T., Nikiforow, N., & Wagener, S. (2020). Determinants of information system quality and data quality in management accounting. *Journal of Management Control, 31,* 97–121.

Langley, M. A. (2019). Success in disruptive times: Expanding the value delivery landscape to address the high cost of low performance. *Project Management Institute,* 1–36.

Maloney, S. (2020). 7 things software leaders should know about artificial intelligence. *Tiempo,* 1–6.

Mikhalchuk, O. (2020). The future of quality assurance industry: Latest software testing trends 2021. *Forte Group,* 1–2.

Narayan, V. (2018). The role of AI in software engineering and testing. *International Journal of Technical Research and Applications, 6*(4), 34–36.

Ravichandran, T., & Rai, A. (2000). Quality management in systems development: An organizational system perspective. *MIS Quarterly, 24*(3), 381–415.

Rummens, N., & Sucher, R. (1989). CASE: Competitive edge. *Systems International, 17*(3), 31–34.

Saratkar, A. N. (2019). An article on importance of software technologies in business and management science. *International Journal of Engineering Applied Sciences and Technology*, *4*(4), 291–294.

Schatsky, D., & Bumb, S. (2020). AI is helping to make better software. *Deloitte*, 1–5.

Tam, C., Moura, E. J., Oliveira, T., & Varajao, J. (2020). The factors influencing the success of on-going agile software development projects. *International Journal of Project Management*, *38*, 165–176.

Williamson, M. (1990). Getting a handle on CASE. *CIO Magazine*, *3*(7), 42–51.

Wilson, K. (2007). What's new in Microsoft Project 2007?: Advantages and benefits of upgrading from Microsoft Project 2000/2003 to Microsoft Project 2007, 1–5. Retrieved from http://www.epmconnect.com/Project%20Professional%20Documents/What's%20New%20In%20Project%202007.pdf. Accessed on January 3, 2017.

Zhao, Y., Li, Y., Zhang, X., Geng, G., Zhang, W., & Sun, Y. (2019). A survey of networking applications applying the software defined networking concept based on machine learning. *IEEE Access*, *2*, 95397–95408.

# 3

# THE IMPORTANCE OF
# PEOPLE IN THE SOFTWARE
# DEVELOPMENT PROCESS

The effect of software development tools on the overall software quality can be considered marginal due to the human-centric nature of software development. Consequently, the benefits of development tools may not be fully realized without knowledgeable, qualified, capable and committed human resource (Chiang & Mookerjee, 2004).

There are many personnel involved in the development and delivery of software products. They are the project sponsor, project managers, project steering committee members, system analyst, network administrator, interface design expert, database administrator, project team members, users and the software developers. The role and responsibility of the software developer will be addressed in this chapter, followed by the role and contribution of other key personnel.

The skills required for each job do not remain static but change with changing technology (Frank et al., 2019). For example, software developers may require more social skills because those skills are difficult to automate. So, while AI and ML are helpful developmental tools along the software development life cycle, they do not negate the need for experienced, committed and skilled software developers, especially with social skills.

### Software Developers

It is imperative that software developers possess a high degree of social skills. Social skills (soft skills) are defined as a person's ability to understand, socially interact, control and read effectively to fulfil an objective (Baron & Markman, 2000). Social skills represent the ability to work in teams, facilitate effective communication, interpersonal competencies, adaptability and knowledge sharing, promote trust, avoid communication breakdowns and facilitate reasonable project expectations and collaborative problem solving (Kerzner & Kerzner, 2017). Social skills include the following traits – leadership, confidence, creativity, compromising and a willingness to solve any issues or conflicts that arise (Zaman et al., 2019). The benefits of social skills are that they can enhance group efficiency and reduce coordination costs (Zaman et al., 2019).

Technical skills (hard skills), on the other hand, are the abilities and knowledge needed to perform specific tasks. It typically requires the use of certain tools and the know-how to effectively use those tools. It meets the requirements of business processes and developmental tools (Zaman et al., 2019). In software development, technical skills are critical for writing codes. The two most important technical skills required by software developers are coding ability and quality of work (Zhou et al., 2018). Coding ability is concerned with the individual's proficiency in coding and is measured by the number of projects owned and the number and frequency of quality issues raised in the relevant fora (Zhou et al., 2018). Quality of work is concerned with the effectiveness and viability of the code that an individual produces and it can be measured by the number of accepted commits (version control) and inclusion of test cases. In the final analysis, both social and technical skills are very desirable (Zhou et al., 2018), because complex decision-making under vast uncertainty is at the heart of today's society (Ernst, 2021). Hence, the success of software projects is dependent on the developer's technical and social skills (Kerzner & Kerzner, 2017).

Highly competent software developers with both social and technical skills are in high demand (Jia, Chen & Du, 2017). As a result, they can demand high salaries. A survey revealed that the US is the world's top-paying country, with an average gross annual salary of US$113,419 for software developers (SalaryExpert, 2022). It also found that software developers in Trinidad and Tobago and Jamaica are earning gross annual salaries of US$27,161 and US$24,939, respectively, as shown in Table 3.1. The difference in annual salary is US$88,480 (US$113,419–US$24,939). It is important to note that one of the major considerations in making a career choice is the salary earned. Based on the close proximity of the US to Jamaica, a number

**Table 3.1**  Software Developers' Average Salary Worldwide by Salary Expert (2022)

| NUMBER | CLASSIFICATION OF COUNTRY | COUNTRY | SALARY IN US$ |
|---|---|---|---|
| 1 | Developed economies | US | $113,419.00 |
| 2 | | Australia | $98,659.61 |
| 3 | | Germany | $96,239.70 |
| 4 | | Norway | $95,959.71 |
| 5 | | Denmark | $94,228.34 |
| 6 | | Canada | $92,605.79 |
| 7 | Developing economies | Brazil | $30,721.03 |
| 8 | | Trinidad and Tobago | $27,161.99 |
| 9 | | Jamaica | $24,939.07 |
| 10 | | Mexico | $24,014.36 |

of software developers in Jamaica might be tempted to seek employment in the US in pursuit of higher salaries.

Table 3.1 shows the wide disparity in salary between developed economies like the US, Australia, Germany and Canada and developing countries like Brazil, Trinidad and Tobago and Jamaica. This salary divide can also act as a catalyst for Jamaican software developers to migrate to the US, coupled with the fact that there is a vast Jamaican diaspora in the US that can offer support to migrant software developers. This migration to the US can create a void in the pool of software developers in Jamaica to successfully manage software projects. It is said that "the skills of developers have a great influence on the quality of the software product and the success of software projects" (Jia et al., 2017).

The agile paradigm emphasizes the importance of people in software development (Cockburn & Highsmith, 2001). Proponents of this view suggest that the competence and contribution of the people involved in software development can impact the quality of the delivered product (Torrecilla-Salinasa et al., 2016). Competence and contribution encompass both technical and social skills. In this book, *competence* refers to project management skills, knowledge of software development methods, software engineering skills and the faithful execution of software practices that are brought to bear on the project. *Contribution* describes the levels of input by project team members towards the successful execution of the project.

It is expected that both the competence and contribution of key stakeholders like software developers and project managers can impact the outcome of software projects, especially in developing countries where there are human resource shortages (Fiestas & Sinha, 2011). It is asserted that if developers are knowledgeable and capable, the possibility exists that the delivered software will be of high quality (Duggan & Reichgelt, 2006). It was further stated that knowledgeable developers are better able to observe sources of inconsistencies, duplication and defects, and take the appropriate corrective actions.

Good collaboration skills among developers can positively enhance coding abilities, as well as enhance the quality of software code (Zhou et al., 2018). In a study conducted in 2000, people skills and contribution were found to be the most important factors over process and technology (Kaltio & Kinnula, 2000). Thus, it is expected that people skills will have a positive impact on software quality.

In addition to developers, users are also critical to the development of high-quality software products and, by extension, the implementation of successful software projects. Users are the ones who are aware of the requirements, features and functionalities of the proposed software product. They must be able to articulate the appropriate requirements of the software product and the developers must be able to understand and assimilate the ideas of the users and design the required software product.

### Users

Keen and committed users can champion and influence the development of cost-effective and high-quality software products. A quality software product is defined as the extent to which the deliverable meets the established standards at the time when it is shipped to the end-user (Konchar & Sanvido, 1998). Developers play a key role on the technical side and users play a key role on the market side. It is important that this collaboration is forged during the early stages of software development because it allows the early detection of flaws/errors and identification of more accurate user requirements, avoids costly features that users may not want and cannot use, improves the level of software product acceptance and reduces development time. Consequently, based on the synergy there is a natural desire to bring developers and users (customers) close together to increase the likelihood of delivering high-quality software products. The probability of adoption and usage tend to be high with the delivery of high-quality software products. The delivery of high-quality software products can enhance swift travel along the diffusion of new software products.

Individuals (users) in both developed and developing economies respond differently to new software features and products. There are five types of adopters for products, namely innovators, early adopters, early majority, late majority and laggards (Rogers, 1995). The diffusion of innovation theory was developed to explain how, why and at what rate new ideas and technology spread. The net result of this diffusion is that individuals adopt a new idea, behaviour or product (Rogers, 1995). The characteristics of each group are highlighted below.

1. Innovators – These are people who want to be the first to try the innovation. They are venturesome and interested in new ideas. These people are very willing to take risks and are often the first to develop new ideas. Very little, if anything, needs to be done to appeal to these individuals.
2. Early Adopters – These people are opinion leaders. They enjoy leadership roles and embrace change opportunities. They are already aware of the need to change and so are very comfortable adopting new ideas. They do not need information to convince them to change.
3. Early Majority – These people are rarely leaders, but they do adopt new ideas before the average person. They, typically, need to see evidence that the innovation works before they are willing to adopt it. Strategies to appeal to this population include success stories and evidence of the innovation's effectiveness.
4. Late Majority – These people are sceptical of change and will only adopt an innovation after it has been tried, tested and proven by the majority. Strategies to appeal to this population include information on how many other people have tried the innovation and have adopted it successfully.
5. Laggards – These people are bound by tradition and very conservative. They are very sceptical of change and are the hardest group to adopt new technologies. Strategies to appeal to this population include convincing statistics regarding the benefits of the software product, as well as pressure from people in the other adopter groups.

The goal is to reach out to all potential users (innovations, early adopters, early majority, late majority and laggards) in an attempt to create individuals' satisfaction or the creation of business value, and ultimately project success.

From the user's perspective, a successful project is one that is finished in minimum time, at the lowest cost and with the best quality (Arditi & Gunaydin, 1997). In addition, it is widely agreed that "The success factor of software heavily depends on whether the software product is able to fulfil the expectations of the intended users" (Alvertis et al., 2016, p. 1). Consequently, detailed planning, coordination, communication and execution are necessary between the user and the software developer.

The COVID-19 pandemic has forced many individuals to adopt a paradigm shift in the execution of daily tasks. It has also caused many non-software firms to accelerate their digital transformation strategies to continue to meet the changing needs of their customers. This shift has resulted in significant growth in the global software industry. The industry is forecasted to grow at a rate of 11.7% annually up to 2030, due in part to the advent of work-from-home, e-commerce and online learning. This has led to an increased demand for software products.

### Biz/Dev and Dev/Ops Concepts

Software development has been characterized by critical disconnects among project planning, development and implementation (Fitzgerald & Stol, 2015). These disconnects have led to the concepts of business strategy and software development (BizDev) and software development and operations (DevOps). As shown in Figure 3.1, BizDev is the link between business strategy and software development which must be continually assessed and improved. Likewise,

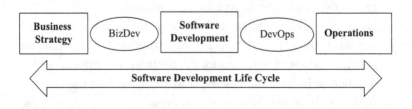

**Figure 3.1**   The holistic view of business, development and operations.

DevOps recognizes that the integration between software development and its operational deployment needs to be a continuous one (Fitzgerald & Stol, 2015).

In general, the top management of organizations develops strategies for growth and establishes key performance indicators to monitor the performance of these strategies. However, various challenges are encountered along the journey, like increased competition, increased operational costs and reduced profits. Most organizations respond to these challenges with software products. Likewise, individuals seek software products to provide various utilities and satisfaction. For example, the six aircraft crew on the Airbus A400Mlas cargo plane in May 2015 had expected to deliver the cargo safely within a reasonable time to the intended customer. However, a software error in the aircraft caused a fatal crash in Spain. Thus, the crew was unable to achieve their goal and the customer was unable to reap the benefit of the expected cargo. Similarly, in the case of the newly designed FaceTime software error that exposed millions of iPhone users to eavesdropping, these users simply wanted the use of their iPhones to transact legitimate communication transactions instead of having their privacy violated.

BizDev is a decision-making approach which operates on the principle that long-term success can only be achieved by establishing a seamless connection between business operations and technology. The goal of BizDev is to pursue opportunities for long-term growth and development by working closely with sales, marketing, product development and information technology departments. It focuses on understanding the needs, wants and expectations of customers, and building long-term relationships on the basis of trust and integrity. In addition, it seeks to align information technology investment with business processes and outcomes and takes a strategic look at business development, designs the right software product and creates customer satisfaction and business value.

On the other hand, DevOps is the collaboration between software developers and operations personnel (users). DevOps is the practice of bringing development and operations teams together to shorten the software development life cycle with faster releases and provide continuous delivery of high-quality software products. It is the union of people, process and technology with the intention to continually provide value to customers. By adopting a DevOps culture, these high-performing teams are better able to respond to customer needs and build software products that provide satisfaction and value. This approach enables departments that formerly operated in individual silos to now coordinate and collaborate to produce more reliable and high-quality software products. Figure 3.1 outlines the relationship among business strategy, software development and operations.

A large part of software quality challenges takes place at the early stages of requirement definition and software design (Yates & Shaller, 1990). In an effort to improve the communication between developers and users at the requirement management stage of the software development cycle, a DevOps approach is recommended. However, it is important to note that the concept of DevOps can be practised in both developed and developing economies, thus minimizing the divide between developed and developing economies.

Expressed differently, DevOps is the streamlining of the activities of software development and operations. It emphasizes the collaboration between software developers and operations personnel. This collaboration assists in shortening the time for development, testing and deployment without compromising quality.

The introduction of these concepts (BizDev and DevOps) is even more important in today's environment in which more complex, safety-critical and data-intensive software products are being developed, often by distributed teams in which collaboration is necessary (Zhou et al., 2018). As a result, a tight and well-established connection is required between development and execution to ensure that errors are detected and fixed early in the software development life cycle (Fitzgerald & Stol, 2015). Hence, a holistic approach is necessary in software development. The project manager plays a key role in coordinating and bringing the project activities together from requirements management to evolution/maintenance.

### Project Managers

No matter the extent of care that project managers exercise to plan, schedule and identify project risks, the success of the project is dependent on the project manager's ability to balance the different interests of key stakeholders to achieve the best outcome (Vijay & Verma, 2018). Stakeholders of each project (project sponsors, software developers, network administrators, users, etc.) have their own interests, conflicting motivations and hidden agendas. This is intensified by the fact that project members are coming from different countries (distributed teams) with different values, attitudes and beliefs.

The project sponsor, for example, is interested in value for his/her investment while the project team members might be keen on high remuneration for tasks completed regardless of the quality of work done. This tension is explained by the agency theory which is defined as "a contract under which one or more persons (the principal(s)) engage another person (the agent) to perform some service on their behalf which involves delegating some decision-making authority to the agent" (Jensen & Meckling, 1976, p. 4). The theory goes further to state that the relationships between the principals and agents could become discordant if both parties seek to maximize their own self-interest (Mitnick, 2006). There is reasonable ground that the agent will not always act in the principal's best interests because of unaligned goals and objectives (Jensen & Meckling, 1976).

It is reasonable to theorize that conflicts may occur during the planning and execution of projects because project teams are composed of individuals with diverse knowledge and experiences (Chen, 2006). Furthermore, conflicts tend to vary along the project life cycle (Jehn & Mannix, 2001). People management factors rather than technical issues are the main determinants of project success (Jehn & Mannix, 2001).

The agency theory has been used in a number of disciplines since its inception (Jehn & Mannix, 2001). It is used to explain relationships in disciplines such as economics (Sappington, 1991), information systems (Mahaney & Lederer, 2011), supply chain management (Zsidisin & Ellram, 2003) and project management (Forsythe et al., 2015). In project management research, the theory is used to explain the relationship between the principal and the agent, when the agent has been engaged and empowered by the principal to make decisions and to act on his behalf (Basu & Lederer, 2011). Essentially, when ownership and control are separated, a number of problems may arise and the agency theory can be applied to explain the various nuances during the execution of the project (Cuevas-Rodriguez et al., 2012).

The underlying assumption of the agency theory is that the agent is basically a selfish opportunist individual who, unless monitored closely, will exploit the principal (Miller & Whitford, 2007). The theory attempts to address two issues. The first issue concerns cooperating parties not necessarily sharing the same interest and common goals (Eisenhardt, 1989). This difference can manifest itself into information asymmetry between the principal and the agent, where one party is better informed than the other, which, most likely, is the agent (Schieg, 2008). In most cases, the agent is in possession of more and better-quality information than the principal. This is so because the agent is usually more knowledgeable about the domain of the project (in this case software development) and is immersed in the day-to-day execution of the project and so has more information than the principal. As a result, the information-rich party (the agent) can opportunistically operate with self-interest rather than in the interest of the other party (the principal) or in the interest of the intended goals of the project. In an effort to curtail this tendency, the principal usually introduces contractual mechanisms to govern the project such as frequent visits, audits and regular reports (Fama & Jensen, 1983).

Prior studies have discovered that increased monitoring promotes the likelihood of the principal receiving information that is less asymmetrical (Fayezi et al., 2012). Another study found that monitoring can lead to project success, as monitoring reduces privately held information (Mahaney & Lederer, 2003). However, these measures can increase the project cost.

This concern is compounded by the second problem of agency cost. Agency cost is described as the sum of the monitoring expenses incurred by the principal (Jensen & Meckling, 1976). In other words, it is the financial costs and implications arising from the difference in interests between the principal and the agent (Lyonnet du Moutier, 2010). It is important to note that the more aligned the interests of the principal and the agent, the higher the likelihood that the agent will work in the principal's interest (Cuevas-Rodriguez et al., 2012). However, an overly structured control and monitoring process may hinder the chance of project success (Muller & Turner, 2005).

Asymmetric information may lead to mistrust and opportunistic behaviour, which can increase the risk profile of the project (Ceric, 2012).

The varied risk profiles of the principal and the agent can lead to different actions being taken or different decisions being made in the execution of the project.

In the midst of these tensions, it is the role and responsibility of the project manager to balance these various interests, as well as making sure that the project is delivered on time, within budget and with zero or minimum bugs. The project manager is the person who has the overall responsibility for the successful initiation, planning, design, execution, monitoring, controlling and closure of a project as outlined below. The project manager's responsibilities are to:

- plan and develop the project idea;
- define the project scope;
- plan and sequence activities;
- develop the project schedule;
- plan human and physical resources;
- estimate time;
- estimate cost (develop the project budget);
- create and lead the team;
- set deadlines, monitor and report on the project's progress;
- manage and control conflicts;
- promote team building;
- ensure stakeholders' satisfaction;
- manage and control risks;
- control quality and benefits realization;
- create and archive relevant documentation; and
- evaluate project performance

The current trend is for software to be developed by distributed teams (Zhou et al., 2018). As a result, successful projects are dependent on well-formed and well-composed teams led by capable, competent and committed project managers (Qamar & Malik, 2020).

In this highly uncertain, dynamic and globalized environment, firms are embarking upon very complex projects due to sophisticated project scope, multi-organizational context and emerging new technologies (Nonino et al., 2018). So even the most carefully planned projects can fall apart if there are improper people skills (Kerzner & Kerzner, 2017). Hence, project managers need excellent people and technical skills.

However, in the midst of the earlier mentioned internal issues (within the project and the organization), project managers must be aware of and respond to various external issues. Major external issues are the constraints and nuances being experienced in the originating country where the software product is developed. These constraints, norms and nuances can impact the outcome of software projects, both positively and negatively. In this book, the originating countries are situated in the Caribbean, the countries of which are classified as developing economies. Hence, the term 'developing economies' will be used throughout the book in reference to the Caribbean.

### Developing Economies

The originating countries discussed in this book are Barbados, Guyana, Jamaica and Trinidad and Tobago, which will be referred to as developing economies. A developing economy is a country with a relatively low standard of living, an underdeveloped industrial base and a moderate to low human development index (HDI). The World Economic Situation and Prospects classifies all countries of the world into three broad categories, namely developed economies, economies in transition and developing economies, which are intended to reflect certain economic conditions. Because the broad categories can be fuzzy, there are sub-groups within each category. For example, the geographic regions for developing economies are Africa, East Asia, Western Asia, South Asia and Latin America and the Caribbean.

The characteristics of developing economies, in general, are low per capita income, excessive dependence on agriculture, low level of capital formation, rapid population growth, high rate of unemployment and low level of human capital (Agarwal, 2022; Sumiyana, 2020).

### *Low per Capita Income*

Low per capita income results from low levels of productivity, low savings and low investments. Low savings and investment mean that the average person does not earn enough income to invest or save. In general, most people spend whatever they earn. As a result, this creates a cycle of poverty that most people in the population struggle to overcome. The low levels of productivity are caused by low performance in production (especially agriculture), lack of technological progress, human resource constraints and rapid population growth.

### Excessive Dependence on Agriculture

Most developing economies are generally predominantly agricultural. About 30–50% of the national income comes from agriculture. This excessive dependence on agriculture is the result of a lack of modern industrial growth.

### Low Level of Capital Formation

Capital formation, also known as net investment, is a term used to describe the net *capital accumulation* during an accounting period for a particular country. It is a measure of the net additions of the capital stock of a country in an accounting period. The low level of capital formation in most developing economies is due to the lack of tendency to invest and the low propensity to save. Because the per capita income is low, most expenditure is focused on satisfying the bare necessities of life, leaving a very small margin of income for capital accumulation.

### Rapid Population Growth

In most developing economies, either the population growth rate is high or the population is large. The increase in the population is high because of high birth rates and reduced death rates through improved healthcare. The disadvantages of rapid population growth are increased burden on the economy, more exploitation of natural resources, deforestation, increased pollution, higher unemployment and more competition for survival.

### High Unemployment Rate

The unemployment rate is the proportion of unemployed persons in the labour force. The unemployment rate does not impact only jobless individuals in the society. It affects the disposable income of families, erodes the purchasing power of individuals, creates job insecurity, diminishes employees' morale, promotes social unrest, increases poverty and reduces the production output of nations.

*Low Levels of Human Capital*

Education, health and skills are major determinants of economic development. There is a great disparity in the human development index (HDI) between developed and developing economies, where the education and skill levels in developing economies are much lower in comparison with developed economies. In general, developing economies lack the human capital necessary for economic development. Lack of education impacts the knowledge and skills of individuals. Lack of education and skills makes individuals less adaptable to change and lowers their ability to plan, organize and manage effectively. These traits can lower the ability of individuals in developing economies to be change agents and wealth creators.

In summary, there are human, financial and infrastructure constraints in developing economies in contrast to developed economies (Chowdhury & Audretsch, 2019). These constraints can curtail the ability to successfully execute software projects. For example, the lack of finance can lead to a lack of investment in required software development tools. Table 3.2 outlines the characteristics of developed versus developing economies (Chen et al., 2006).

**Table 3.2**    The Characteristics of Developed and Developing Economies

| FACTOR | DEVELOPED ECONOMIES | DEVELOPING ECONOMIES |
|---|---|---|
| Economy | Economy growing at a constant rate, productivity increasing and a high standard of living | Economy not growing or increasing in productivity and low standard of living |
| Technical Staff | Has outsourcing abilities and financial resources to outsource<br>Staff are able to define requirements for development | Does not have staff with the requisite technical skills, or has very limited in-house staff (software developers)<br>Does not have local outsourcing abilities and rarely has the financial ability to outsource<br>Staff may be unable to define specific requirements |
| Infrastructure | Good current infrastructure<br>High internet access for employees and citizens | Weak infrastructure<br>Low internet access for employees and citizens |
| Government Officers | Decent computer literacy and dedication of resources<br>Many do not place e-government at a high priority | Low computer literacy and low dedication of resources<br>Many do not place e-government at a high priority due to a lack of knowledge on the issue |

## The Caribbean

The Caribbean countries, which are classified as developing economies, conform to most of the characteristics stated above, as well as
having a relatively large infrastructure deficit that has affected their
economic growth (Caribbean Development Bank, 2014). There is reference to resource poverty in finance, human resources and equipment in the Caribbean region. It is stated that there is a heavy reliance
on imported software products in the region, yet there are foreign
exchange shortages to purchase needed supplies. In addition, there
is a scarcity of technical personnel due to migration (unavailability of
software specialists), coupled with low productivity and aversion to
change (Chevers et al., 2016).

The Caribbean is a region of the Americas consisting of the
Caribbean Sea and its islands. The region is strategically located to
the southeast of North America, east of Central America and north-
west of South America. About half of its population resides in North
America, Canada and the United Kingdom.

There are a number of common characteristics shared among the
different economies of the Caribbean region. In general, these small
economies lack natural resources and are subjected to natural disasters
from volcanoes to hurricanes, which can lead to a loss of much-needed
physical infrastructure, valuable capital and irreplaceable lives. For
example, in 2004, Hurricane Ivan caused more than J$360 million
worth of damage to property and infrastructure in Jamaica. Instead
of servicing debt or investing in capacity building of the human and
physical resources, the scarce funds had to be used to restore the country to a state prior to the hurricane.

Small economies in the Caribbean also depend heavily on agricultural production, fishing and tourism, and rely on strong trade
relationships. In addition, they are highly dependent on imports
from the US and other developed economies and there is usually a trade imbalance, skewed more towards imports instead of
exports. Earning needed foreign exchange is critical to the sustainability of many Caribbean islands. The countries in the region
that possess a reasonable foreign exchange reserve are better able
to acquire the latest software development tools and invest in the
latest technologies.

It is important to invest in technologies in an effort to boost the competitiveness of nations, as well as the well-being of the citizens. The Network Readiness Index (NRI) is a key indicator of how countries are doing in the digital world. More specifically, the Network Readiness Index measures how well an economy is using information and communication technologies (ICTs) to exploit opportunities and improve its performance in measures such as competitiveness, productivity and standard of living.

The world is on the eve of another era in which digital, biological and physical technologies are being brought together in powerful combinations. The NRI is an indication of how ready each country is to reap the benefits of this global revolution. The index is a composite score consisting of four pillars. The four pillars are technology, people, governance and impact. The technology pillar seeks to assess the level of technology that is absolutely necessary for a country's participation in the global economy. The measured dimensions are access, content and future technologies. The people pillar seeks to assess if the population and organizations have the access, resources and skills to use the technology productively. The unit of observation for this measure is at the individual, business and government levels. The governance pillar seeks to capture how conducive the national environment is for a country's participation in the network economy, based on issues of trust, regulation and inclusion. The measured dimensions are trust, regulation and inclusion. Finally, the impact pillar seeks to assess the economic, social and human impact of participation in the network economy. The measured dimensions are the economy, quality of life and the contribution of the sustainable development goals (SDGs).

The NRI has been measuring the information and communication technology readiness of around 130 countries worldwide based on the readiness index. These 130 economies collectively account for almost 95% of the global gross domestic product (GDP). Table 3.3 outlines the network readiness ranking of a few developed and developing economies (Dutta & Lanvin, 2021). The developing economies in the Caribbean are Jamaica, the Dominican Republic and Trinidad and Tobago. From the table, it can be deduced that the Caribbean islands are in the 50th percentile of the readiness index and the two major areas requiring improvement are people and technology (101/130 and

**Table 3.3**  Network Readiness Index 2021 by Dutta and Lanvin (2021)

| DEVELOPED / DEVELOPING ECONOMY | COUNTRY | RANK (2021) | SCORE | GREATEST SCOPE FOR IMPROVEMENT |
|---|---|---|---|---|
| Developed Economies | Netherlands | 1 | 82.06 | People (7/130) |
| | United States | 4 | 81.09 | Impact (16/130) |
| | Singapore | 7 | 80.01 | Governance (12/130) |
| | United Kingdom | 10 | 76.60 | People (16/130) |
| | Canada | 11 | 76.48 | Impact (20/130) |
| | Australia | 13 | 74.96 | Impact (23/130) |
| Developing Economies | Jamaica | 74 | 47.95 | People (101/130) |
| | Dominican Republic | 82 | 45.33 | Technology (99/130) |
| | Trinidad and Tobago | 85 | 44.80 | Impact (90/130) |

99/130, respectively). This illustrates the divide between developed and developing economies.

Similarly, the global Internet Penetration Rate (IPR) is in alignment with the NRI in terms of the developed versus the developing economies. The IPR is the percentage of the total population of a given country that uses the internet. An internet user is anyone currently with the capacity to use the internet. The measured dimensions are (1) having access to an internet connection point; and (2) having the basic knowledge required to use the software product. Table 3.4 outlines the ranking between developed and developing economies (International Telecommunication Union, 2020). Again, the developing economies are represented by the Caribbean islands. The penetration rates in the developed economies range from 96.8% to 83.7%, while the Caribbean islands range from 81.5% to 37.3%, which established that there is also a digital divide.

Based on the scores of the NRI and the IPR, project managers in the Caribbean might find it difficult to consistently develop and deliver high-quality software products due to the many constraints being experienced in this region. Some of the constraints are not having access to relevant and needed technologies, not being able to purchase the latest technologies or not having personnel with the requisite skills to use the latest technologies. This is exacerbated by the data which shows that the Caribbean loses 70% of its tertiary graduates annually due to migration (International Monetary Fund, 2006).

The complexity of software projects, combined with the need to integrate business strategy, development and operations, requires

**Table 3.4**   Internet Penetration Rate by the International Telecommunication Union (2020)

| DEVELOPED / DEVELOPING ECONOMY | COUNTRY | PENETRATION RATE (2020) (%) | POPULATION |
|---|---|---|---|
| Developed Economies | United Kingdom | 96.8 | 67,141,684 |
| | United States | 95.5 | 327,096,265 |
| | Netherlands | 93.1 | 17,059,560 |
| | Canada | 91.6 | 37,064,562 |
| | Australia | 85.0 | 24,898,152 |
| | Singapore | 83.7 | 5,757,499 |
| Developing Economies | Barbados | 81.5 | 286,641 |
| | Trinidad and Tobago | 76.2 | 1,389,843 |
| | Dominican Republic | 65.8 | 10,627,141 |
| | Saint Lucia | 50.0 | 181,889 |
| | Jamaica | 48.0 | 2.934,847 |
| | Guyana | 37.3 | 779,006 |

software developers with specialized skills (Batistic & Kenda, 2018). Software projects in developing economies usually differ greatly from those in developed countries for various reasons. Most developing economies face different levels of the digital divide due to underdeveloped technology infrastructure and technical know-how (Chen et al., 2006; Heeks, 2002). To further compound the problem, the software industry is characterized by a high delivery rate of products, a high rate of process innovations, significant experience in adopting innovative practices for designing and developing products, high knowledge intensity and rapidly shrinking products (Nambisan, 2002).

It is important to note that software projects in developing economies usually fail before being formally introduced to their users (Badewi & Shehab, 2016). However, the cost of software development is decreasing due to the proliferation of open-source software products and cloud-based services, but competition has been increasing due to the lowering of entry barriers (Alvertis et al., 2016).

The increased global competition among software development firms has made it difficult for firms in the Caribbean due to the constraints expressed earlier. The constraints include resource poverty in finance, scarcity of technical personnel due to migration, aversion to change and relatively large infrastructure deficit. Combined with these constraints is the fact that most software development firms in the Caribbean can be classified as small in comparison with their counterparts in developed countries. Based on their size and constraints it might be a challenge for them to adopt the full-blown and well-established process maturity frameworks being utilized by firms in developed economies.

### Size of Firms

Micro, small and medium-sized firms play a central role in the economic development of nations by addressing the challenges of poverty, inequality and job creation. Small businesses are an important source of employment. They represent around 90% of all global businesses and 50% of worldwide employment (Carter, 2022). In fact, they are considered the engine of economic growth and development. However, they frequently experience difficulty in obtaining capital or credit, especially in the early start-up phase. In general, they rely on internal funds, or cash from friends and relatives to operate and sustain the business. This restriction can curtail access to new technologies and innovation. In this book, small firms are defined as those with ten to less than 50 employees and an annual turnover of 10 million euros (European Commission, 2005).

Based on this definition, most software development firms in the Caribbean would be classified as small firms. Yet, it is difficult to know the precise number of small businesses worldwide, as new entrepreneurs keep entering the market. The current estimate is around 400 million (Carter, 2022). According to Carter (2022) the global statistics of small businesses are as follows.

1. Around 44% of small business owners belong to the Generation X group (39–54 years old).
2. About 53.7% of small business owners have a bachelor's degree or higher.
3. The service industry is the most popular area of enterprise for small business owners.
4. Fifty-six per cent of small business owners struggle to find employees for their businesses.
5. Working overtime is common for small business owners.
6. Sixty-five per cent of entrepreneurs felt they did not have enough capital (cash) to start a business.

7. Ninety-three per cent of business owners calculated a survival rate of around 18 months.
8. Around 65 million firms in developing countries have an unmet financing need of around US$5.2 trillion each year. With the Caribbean and the Middle East, North Africa and the Latin American region having the highest financial gaps.
9. About 50% of small businesses survive more than five years.
10. Seventy-two per cent of small business owners feel optimistic about the future. With 72% growing their online presence and 71% feeling that they survived the COVID-19 pandemic because they invested in digital transformation

In summary, small businesses are the backbone of nations as they make a significant contribution to GDP. As a result, it is imperative that policies, procedures and frameworks be formulated to enhance the growth and sustainability of these firms. Particular focus should be given to those firms in the software development sector which are believed to offer the greatest benefits in terms of digital transformation and a sustainable competitive advantage.

The digital divide between developed and developing countries has led to the migration of qualified software developers to developed countries in search of greater opportunities and higher salaries. This trend has curtailed the growth and development of software development firms in developing countries. In general, these firms can be classified as being small.

However, with the popularity of distributed teams in software development, the effect of such migration can be minimized. In addition, the current trend of Biz/Dev and Dev/Ops can enhance improved idea generation, improved exchange of ideas, improved learning and greater collaboration. Improved collaboration can reduce asymmetric information which can impact the outcome of software projects.

### References

Agarwal, P. (2022). Characteristics of developing economies. *Intelligent Economist*, 1–9.

Alvertis, I., Koussouris, S., Papaspyros, D., Arvanitakis, E., Mouzakitis, S., Franken, S., & Prinz, W. (2016). User involvement in development processes. *Procedia Computer Science*, *97*, 73–83.

Arditi, D., & Gunaydin, H. M. (1997). Total quality management in the construction process. *Internation Journal of Project Management, 15*(4), 235–243.

Badewi, A., & Shehab, E. (2016). The impact of organizational project benefits management governance on ERP project success: Neo-institutional theory perspective. *International Journal of Project Management, 34*(3), 412–428.

Baron, R. A., & Markman, G. D. (2000). Beyond social capital: How social skills can enhance entrepreneurs' success. *Academy of Management Executive, 14*(1), 106–116.

Basu, V., & Lederer, A. L. (2011). Agency theory and consultant management in enterprise resource planning systems implementation. *Data Base for Advances in Information Systems, 42*(3), 10–33.

Batistic, S., & Kenda, R. (2018). Toward a model of socializing project team members: An integrative approach. *International Journal of Project Management, 36*(5), 687–700.

Caribbean Development Bank. (2014). Public-private partnership in the Caribbean: Building on early lessons. *Caribbean Development Bank*, 1–147. Retrieved from https://www.caribank.org/sites/default/files/publication-resources/Booklet-Public-Private-Partnerships-in-the-Caribbean-Building-on-Early-Lessons_0.pdf.

Carter, R. (2022). The ultimate list of small business statistics for 2022. *Findstack*, 1–19.

Ceric, A. (2012). Communication risk in construction projects: Application of principal-agent theory. *Organization, Technology and Management in Construction: An International Journal, 4*(2), 522–533.

Chen, M. H. (2006). Understanding the benefits and detriments of conflict on team creativity process. *Journal Compilation, 15*(1), 105–116.

Chen, H. M., Huang, W., & Ching, R. K. H. (2006). E-Government strategies in developed and developing countries: An implementation framework and case study. *Journal of Global Information Management, 14*(1), 23–46.

Chevers, D. A., Mills, A. M., Duggan, E., & Moore, S. (2016). An evaluation of software development practices among small firms in developing countries - A test of a simplified software process improvement model. *Journal of Global Information Management, 24*(3), 46–71.

Chiang, I. R., & Mookerjee, V. S. (2004). Improving software team productivity. *Communications of ACM, 47*(5), 89–93.

Chowdhury, F., & Audretsch, D. B. (2019). Institutions and entrepreneurship quality. *Entrepreneurship Theory and Practice, 43*(1), 51–81.

Cockburn, A., & Highsmith, J. (2001). Agile software development: The people factor. *Computer, 34*(11), 131–133.

Cuevas-Rodriguez, G., Gomez-Mejia, L. R., & Wiseman, R. M. (2012). Has agency theory run its course? Making the theory more flexible to inform the management of reward systems. *Corporate Governance: An International Review, 20*(6), 526–546.

Duggan, E. W., & Reichgelt, H. J. P. M. (2006). *Measuring information systems delivery quality*. Hershey, PA: Idea Group, Inc.

Dutta, S., & Lanvin, B. (2021). The Network Readiness Index 2021: Shaping the global recovery. *Portulans Institute*, 1–278.

Eisenhardt, K. M. (1989). Agency theory: An assessment and review. *Academy of Management Review, 14*(1), 57–74.

Ernst, E. (2021). The economics of artificial intelligence: An agenda by Ajay Agrawal, Joshua Gans and Avi Goldfarb. *Pluto Journals, 37*(2), 191–197.

European Commission, T. (2005). The new SME definition: User guide and model declaration. *Enterprise and Industry Publications*, 1–51.

Fama, E. F., & Jensen, M. C. (1983). Agency problems and residual claims. *Journal of Law and Economics, 26*(2), 327–349.

Fayezi, S., O'Loughlin, A., & Zutshi, A. (2012). Agency theory and supply chain management: A structured literature review. *Supply Chain Management: An international Journal, 17*(5), 556–570.

Fiestas, I., & Sinha, S. (2011). Constraints to private investment in the poorest developing countries - A review of the literature. *Nathan*, 1–34.

Fitzgerald, B., & Stol, K. (2017). Continuous software engineering: A roadmap and agenda. *The Journal of System and Software, 123*, 176–189.

Forsythe, P., Sankaran, S., & Biesenthal, C. (2015). How far can BIM reduce information asymmetry in the Australian construction context. *Project Management Journal, 46*(3), 75–87.

Frank, M. R., Autor, D., Beesen, J. E., Brynjolfsson, E., Cebrian, M. D., Deming, D. J., Feldman, M., … & Youn, H. (2019). Toward understanding the impact of artificial intelligence on labor. *Perspective, 116*(14), 6531–6539.

Heeks, R. (2002). Information systems and developing countries: Failure, success, and local improvisations. *The Information Society, 18*, 101–112.

International Monetary Fund. (2006, February 20). Major Brain Drain. *Jamaica Daily Gleaner*, 1–36. Retrieved from https://gleaner.newspaperarchive.com/kingston-gleaner/2006-02-20/.

International Telecommunication Union. (2020). List of countries by number of internet users 2020, 1–11. Retrieved from https://lafibre.info/images/ipv6/202010_wikipedia_list_of_countries_by_number_of_internet_users.pdf.

Jehn, K. A., & Mannix, E. A. (2001). The dynamic nature of conflict: A longitudinal study of intra-group conflict and group performance. *Academy of Management Journal, 44*, 238–251.

Jensen, M. C., & Meckling, W. H. (1976). Theory of the firm: Managerial behaviour, agency costs and ownership structure. *Journal of Financial Economics, 3*(4), 305–360.

Jia, J., Chen, Z., & Du, X. (2017). *Understanding soft skills requirement for mobile applications developers.* Paper presented at the IEEE International Conference on Software Quality in Guangzhou, China.

Kaltio, T., & Kinnula, A. (2000). Deploying the defined SW process. *Software Process: Improvement and Practice, 5*(1), 65–83.

Kerzner, H., & Kerzner, H. R. (2017). *Project management: A systems approach to planning, scheduling, and controlling.* New York: Wiley.

Konchar, M., & Sanvido, V. (1998). Comparison of US project delivery systems. *Journal of Construction Engineering Management, 124*(6), 435–444.

Lyonnet du Moutier, M. (2010). Financing the Eiffel Tower: Project finance and agency theory. *Journal of Applied Finance, 1,* 127–141.

Mahaney, R. C., & Lederer, A. L. (2003). Information systems project management: An agency theory interpretation. *Journal of Systems and Software, 68*(1), 1–9.

Mahaney, R. C., & Lederer, A. L. (2011). An agency theory explanation of project success. *The Journal of Computer Information Systems, 51*(4), 102–113.

Miller, G. J., & Whitford, A. B. (2007). The principal's moral hazard: Constraints on the use of incentives in hierarchy. *Journal of Public Administration Research and Theory, 17*(2), 213–233.

Mitnick, B. M. (2006). Origin of the theory of agency: An account by one of the theory's originators. *University of Pittsburgh,* 1–12.

Muller, R., & Turner, J. R. (2005). The impact of principal-agent relationship and contract type on communication between project owner and manager. *International Journal of Project Management, 5,* 398–403.

Nambisan, S. (2002). Software firm evolution and innovation - orientation. *Journal of Engineering and Technology Management, 19*(2), 141–165.

Nonino, F., Annarelli, A., Gerosa, S., Mosea, P., & Setti, S. (2018). Project management: Driving complexity. *Project Management Institute, 43,* 1–11.

Pinto, J. K., & Slevin, D. P. (1988). Critical success factors across the project life cycle. *Project Management Journal, 19*(3), 67–75.

Qamar, N., & Malik, A. A. (2020). Determining the relative importance of personality traits in influencing software quality and team productivity. *Computing and Informatics, 39,* 994–1021.

Rogers, E. M. (1995). *Diffusion of innovations.* New York, NY: Free Press.

SalaryExpert. (2022). Average software developer salary in 2022. *Economic Research Institute,* 1–3.

Sappington, D. E. (1991). Incentives in principal-agent relationships. *The Journal of Economic Perspectives, 5*(2), 45–66.

Schieg, M. (2008). Strategies for avoiding asymmetric information in construction project management. *Journal of Business Economics and Management, 9*(1), 47–51.

Sumiyana, S. (2020). Different characteristics of the aggregate of accounting earnings between developed and developing countries: Evidence for predicting future GDP. *Journal of International Studies, 13*(1), 58–80.

Torrecilla-Salinasa, C. J., Sedeñoa, J., Escalonaa, M. J., & Mejíasa, M. (2016). Agile, web engineering and capability maturity model integration: A systematic literature review. *Information and Software Technology, 71,* 92–107.

Vijay, K. V. (2018). *The art of positive politics: A key to delivering successful projects.* St. Louis: Multi-Media Publications.

Yates, W. D., & Shaller, D. A. (1990). *Reliability engineering as applied to software.* Paper presented at the Proceedings of Reliability and Maintainability Symposium, Los Angeles, CA.

Zaman, U., Jabbar, Z., Nawaz, S., & Abbas, M. (2019). Understanding the soft side of software projects: An empirical study on the interactive effects of social skills and political skills on complexity - performance relationship. *International Journal of Project Management, 37,* 444–460.

Zhou, C., Kuttal, S. K., & Ahmed, I. (2018). *What makes a good developer? An empirical study of developers' technical and social competencies.* Paper presented at the IEEE Symposium on Visual Languages and Human-Centric Computing in Lisbon, Portugal.

Zsidisin, G. A., & Ellram, L. M. (2003). An agency theory investigation of supply risk management. *Journal of Supply Chain Management, 39*(3), 15–23.

# 4

## LEVERAGE THE NEED FOR PROCESS MATURITY IN SOFTWARE DEVELOPMENT

In order to be competitive and to survive in the software industry, software development firms, both large and small, must develop and deliver high-quality software products (Larrucea et al., 2016). Yet managing the developmental process and delivering high-quality software products has been a challenge for years (Larrucea et al., 2016). These challenges have been manifested in cases of high project failure rates, time overruns and budget overruns. The 2015 Chaos Report found that 44% of software projects were on-budget, 40% on-time and 56% on-target between 2011 and 2015 (Standish Group, 2015). One established approach to overcome these challenges is to achieve a mature process with the application of software process improvement (SPI) programs. Maturity is defined as the degree to which a process is defined, managed, measured and continually improved (Dooley et al., 2001). However, the concept of process maturity and SPI programs will be addressed later in the book.

All software projects experience evolving targets (scope changes), even the very small projects. As a result, the modern definition of a successful project is one that is on-time, on-budget with a satisfactory result (Standish Group, 2015). In contrast to the former definition of being on-time, on-budget and on-target. The modern definition seeks to avoid penalizing a project for having an evolving target. Hence, the modern definition of a successful project is one that is completed within a reasonable estimated time, stayed within budget, and delivered customer and user satisfaction regardless of the original scope. In general, end-users/customers have a clear opinion of the satisfaction level of a delivered software product, whether or not all the features and functions that they asked for at the beginning of the project are realized. In fact, it is widely agreed that 80% of the features in

DOI: 10.1201/9781003388944-4

the average software product are rarely or never used, and the additional features can, most likely, increase cost, increase project risk and reduce software quality, but do not necessarily provide value (Standish Group, 2015).

However, it is important to note that value can only be achieved when the major features of the software product are used. Success can only be achieved at the individual and/or firm level through the utilization of the software product. The Standish Group is an independent international IT research firm which is known for its annual reports on the success of software projects. The 2015 Chaos Report (as shown in Table 4.1) on software project success shows the rate of success as being 29%, challenged projects 52% and failed projects 19% (Standish Group, 2015). Challenged projects are those projects that are late, over budget and/or with less than the required features and functions, while failed projects are those projects that are cancelled prior to completion or delivered and never used. But small firms in developing economies with financial, physical and human constraints do not have the capacity to absorb such failures in comparison with large firms (Fiestas & Sinha, 2011). This divide can severely curtail the competitiveness of small software development firms in the global market.

Even seemingly technically sound and high-quality software products may sometimes fail if they do not prove to be operationally feasible and therefore remain unused (Lyytinen, 1988; Markus & Keil, 1994; Newman & Robey, 1992). However, the likelihood of being successful is much higher when the delivered software product is of high quality.

The delivery of low-quality software products not only impedes the ability of firms to secure local and global contracts but negatively impacts the sustainability of firms (Ingalsbe et al., 2001; Niazi et al., 2010; Serrano et al., 2006; Sulayman et al., 2012). This inability to

**Table 4.1**  Modern Resolution for All Projects

|  | 2011 (%) | 2012 (%) | 2013 (%) | 2014 (%) | 2015 (%) |
| --- | --- | --- | --- | --- | --- |
| Successful | 29 | 27 | 31 | 28 | 29 |
| Challenged | 49 | 56 | 50 | 55 | 52 |
| Failed | 22 | 17 | 19 | 17 | 19 |

secure contracts can lead to the closure of such firms (Niazi et al., 2010) because customers are demanding high-quality software products (Gorla & Lin, 2010; Vasconcellos et al., 2017 ). Furthermore, the ability to win global contracts can facilitate access to needed foreign exchange, especially for small firms in the Caribbean. This, by extension, can lead to economic growth and development of nations. Consequently, the need for quality improvement is a key imperative for the survival and sustainability of firms.

### Software Process Improvement (SPI)

In response to the need for quality improvement, many firms adopt software process improvement (SPI) programs. This is an organizational-level initiative which is described as having the fundamental objective of changing organizational practices in order to improve software product quality (Iversen & Ngwenyama, 2005). The main aim of SPI is to have established practices to improve the software development process which includes obtaining and managing requirements, planning projects, preparing work plans and schedules, decision-making, measuring capabilities and risk-handling (Anees & Agrwal, 2017).

Software process improvement is best achieved through the institutionalization of a comprehensive set of practices to regulate the software delivery activities and establish specific procedures to advance through the development cycle (Duggan & Gibson, 2006). Because the software process is well defined, project managers have reasonable insights into the progress of the project. In outlining the stages of SPI, Humphrey (1989) stated the following four steps:

1. assessing the effectiveness of the existing systems development practices;
2. developing vision and goals;
3. establishing implementation plans to achieve those goals; and
4. instituting a culture of continuous improvement.

Bicego and Kuvaja (1996), in their study, detailed the steps involved in SPI initiatives. They emphasized that an organization's software delivery process is evaluated by a process assessment instrument, which leads to process improvement and capability determination.

Capability determination identifies the maturity and the risk of the process, while process improvement identifies the changes to the process to achieve higher maturity. It is expected that process improvement identifies changes to the process to reduce its 'riskiness' (Bicego & Kuvaja, 1996). This book is centred on the process assessment aspect of SPI.

Therefore, SPI focuses on creating a disciplined, capable and mature process in the software delivery cycle, in an effort to increase the ability to meet the expectations of the market and key stakeholders (Fuggetta, 2000). It is hoped that a disciplined approach and embedded practices like requirements management, software design and implementation, and software validation and evolution should result in better control over the software delivery process (Anees & Agrwal, 2017; Krishnan et al., 2000). It is generally felt in the information systems (IS) community that insufficient attention to software process improvement efforts can negatively impact a firm's ability to produce high-quality software products (Bicego & Kuvaja, 1996; Hasse, 1996).

Empirical evidence indicates that a well-defined software process (through increased levels of process maturity) can significantly influence the quality of the delivered software product (Harter et al., 1998; Khalifa & Verner, 2000; Krishnan & Keller, 1999; Ravichandran & Rai, 2000). Several scholars have posited the benefits of SPI programs (Larrucea et al., 2016; Lee et al., 2016; Niazi et al., 2010; Staples & Niazi, 2008). These benefits include:

- improved software product quality;
- reduced project cycle time – development and delivery time;
- improved return on investment;
- improved customer satisfaction; and
- improved developer productivity.

Furthermore, it is widely believed that people, technology and process are major determinants of software quality (Biro & Messnarz, 2009; Ebert & De Man, 2008; Gorla & Lin, 2010; Seliem et al., 2004). The central belief is that software product quality is influenced by the *people* who are involved in the development process and the usage of the software product, the *technology* used to support its development and the software development *process* that is adopted (SEI, 2010). These determinants singularly or in combination are possible solutions to address the problem of delivering low-quality software products and the high level of software project failures. However, some scholars believe that the quality of the delivered software product relies heavily on the maturity of the software development process (Iqbal et al., 2016; Pane & Sarnob, 2015; SEI, 2010). This view has led to the birth of software process improvement initiatives (Humphrey, 1989). Proponents of this view state: "Everyone realizes the importance of having a motivated, quality work force and the latest technology, but even the finest people can't perform at their best when the process is not understood or operating at its best" (SEI, 2005, p. 9).

Process improvement recommends taking a number of established measures to pave the way towards enhanced software processes (established software development practices) that result in high-quality software being delivered on time, within budget and with the requisite quality features (Iqbal et al., 2016).

### The Capability Maturity Model Integration (CMMI)

The most popular process improvement model to determine the maturity of a firm is the Capability Maturity Model Integration for Development (Odeh et al., 2021; Pane & Sarnob, 2015; Torrecilla-Salinasa et al., 2016). It is commonly called CMMI-Dev. Some of the other models are the capability maturity model (CMM), software process improvement and capability dEtermination (SPICE), personal software process (PSP) and the International Organization for Standardization (ISO). However, the CMMI has become the *de facto* standard for assessing and improving processes and is supported by the Software Engineering Institute (SEI, 2010). The model not only assesses process maturity but also provides a reference point for planning improvement initiatives (SEI, 2010). The CMMI ensures high quality by designing practices that are easily repeatable.

The CMMI is a process improvement model that provides a set of best practices that address productivity, performance and stakeholder satisfaction. The CMMI has two representations which can be adopted by any software development firm that is interested in improving its processes – continuous and staged. Representation allows an organization to pursue different improvement strategies.

The staged representation matures the organization. It uses maturity levels to measure process improvement. This approach divides the process improvement effort into five maturity levels – 1 to 5 – with 5 being the highest level of maturity. Each maturity level has an array of established process practices which an organization will need to implement. Process practices at a lower level form the foundation of process practices at a higher level. In other words, to be assessed at Level 3, the respective organization must have adopted and mastered all seven process practices at Level 2 at a reasonable degree of insti-tutionalization. Figure 4.1 shows the staged representation of the CMMI framework in which firms seek to progress from one maturity level to the next (Paulk et al., 1993; SEI, 2010).

In order to progress from one maturity level to the next, firms must demonstrate compliance with the practices at the lower level. At Level 1, there are no defined software development practices (previ-ously called process areas but now referred to as process practices). Level 1 is ad-hoc in nature and success depends on individual effort. At Level 2, certain basic project management practices are defined such as requirements management, project planning, and project monitoring and control. The practices at this level seek to enhance the ability to repeat earlier successes on projects with similar applications. At Level 3, the practices are well-defined, documented and communi-cated to key personnel. However, quantitative measures are not estab-lished at this level. At Level 4, key performance indicators (measures) are established and measured regarding the software product and the

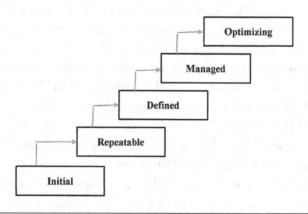

**Figure 4.1**   The maturity levels of CMMI_Staged representation.

development process. At Level 5, the practices are institutionalized, and a culture of continuous improvement prevails. In pursuit of being competitive, firms should seek to improve their software development practices and advance along the maturity continuum (SEI, 2010).

The process practices in each of the maturity levels are as follows.

Level 5 – Causal analysis and resolution (CAR)
    Organizational innovation and development (OID)
Level 4 – Organizational process performance (OPP)
    Quantitative project management (QPM)
Level 3 – Organization process focus (OPF)
    Organization process definition (OPD)
    Organizational training (OT)
    Integrated project management (IPM)
    Risk management (RSKM)
    Requirements development (RD)
    Technical solution (TS)
    Product integration (PI)
    Verification (VER)
    Validation (VAL)
    Decision analysis and resolution (DAR)
Level 2 – Requirements management (REQM)
    Project planning (PP)
    Project monitoring and control (PMC)
    Supplier agreement management (SAM)
    Product and process quality assurance (PPQA)
    Configuration management (CM)
    Measurement and analysis (MA)
Level 1 – There are no process practices at this level

The continuous representation uses capability levels to measure process improvement. This approach is used by organizations that want to improve the capability of specific process practices within the organization. Special emphasis is given to aspects of the organization that are most critical to their business needs. In other words, it provides flexibility for organizations to choose which process practices to emphasize for improvement based on the strategic direction of the organization and/or the specific needs of their customers. For example, a firm may choose to emphasize/master five process practices at

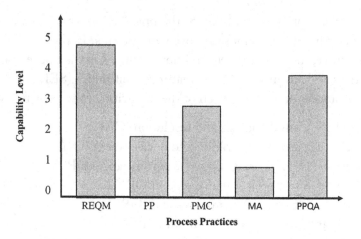

**Figure 4.2**    The CMMI continuous representation.

Level 2. These process practices could be requirements management (REQM), project planning (PP), project monitoring and control (PMC), measurement and analysis (MA), and process and product quality assurance (PPQA), as shown in Figure 4.2. In this case, the firm would seek to master these five process practices and then later seek to master configuration management and supplier agreement management.

A number of obstacles hinder organizations from adopting and implementing CMMI, especially small firms that operate under tight financial and human resources (Montoni et al., 2009; Niazi, 2012; Odeh et al., 2021). Since 1997, in an attempt to increase the adoption of the CMMI, the Software Engineering Institute has developed a series of CMMI versions. Below is the evolution of the various versions from the Capability Maturity Model (CMM) to the CMMI.

- 1993 – CMM for Software V1.1
- 1997 – Software CMM V2.0
- 2000 – CMMI for Development V1.02
- 2002 – CMMI for Development V1.1
- 2006 – CMMI for Development V1.2
- 2010 – CMMI for Development V1.3
- 2018 – CMMI for Development V2.0

The CMMI V2.0 product suite has shifted the framework from a process compliance model to a business performance improvement model (Cong, 2021). The process compliance model is in alignment with the staged representation, while the shift to the business performance improvement model is in alignment with the continuous representation. The guiding philosophy behind this shift is that performance drives process improvements rather than improvements in processes will improve performance. It is a proven set of global best practices that enables organizations to build and benchmark the key capabilities that address their most common business challenges.

The CMMI V2.0 consistently improves business performance for organizations. An analysis of the before and after performance improvement objectives of 95 CMMI-appraised organizations (a total of 735 objectives) in the required CMMI V2.0 Performance Report template showed a 70% achievement success rate (Cong, 2021). The details of the findings are:

1. improved software product quality by 70%;
2. improved developer productivity by 54%;
3. reduced rework by 60%;
4. average improvement in defect containment by 23%; and
5. increased development velocity up to 38%.

Further details of the study showed 61% of the CMMI appraisals recorded came from India (26%), the US (22%) and China (13%). The model is used across a wide range of industries with the top six being financial services, transportation, government/public services, telecommunications, business management and information technology. Nearly 70% of the objectives were met or exceeded, with another 20% having the capability to be met in the future. The top six objectives are software product quality, developer productivity, cost management, schedule management, process adherence and customer satisfaction.

The quality-related objectives represented the biggest performance improvement, with a significant reduction in delivered defects and increased work product quality and increased testing effectiveness. It is important to note that these three categories of quality performance objectives are critical for developmental methods like DevOps and Agile. Improvement in quality performance was achieved, as well as the ability to detect and prevent defects in the development process.

The top three categories of quality-related improvement objectives achieved accounted for 80% of the total quality objectives achieved across the 96 organizations appraised.

With respect to productivity improvement, development velocity, delivery efficiency and effort proportion made up 80% of the measures across the organizations appraised. Development velocity is defined as the amount of product or work product produced per unit effort or time, and this measure is critical for time-to-market (Cong, 2021). Development velocity is directly related to streamlining critical development process performance and process automation such as automated testing, development processes and DevOps.

In terms of cost management, effort variance saw the greatest improvement. Effort variance is defined as the difference in the planned and actual effort as a percentage of planned effort (Cong, 2021). The top five improvement types accounted for 86% as follows: effort variance (48%), cost variance (14%), cost efficiency (12%), cost reduction (7%) and service cost (5%). Cost variance is defined as the difference in planned and actual costs as a percentage of planned costs. Cost efficiency is the act of saving money by changing a process to work in a better way. It is measured by calculating the ratio of the output produced to the cost incurred. Cost reduction is defined as the degree to which actual costs are reduced and service cost is measured based on the service usage costs.

With respect to the schedule performance, meeting milestones and schedule variance were the top two measures, accounting for 74%. Meeting milestones and schedule variance accounted for 50% and 24%, respectively. Meeting milestones is defined as the proportion of target dates (e.g. milestones or delivery dates) that are achieved and schedule variance is the difference in planned and actual dates as a percentage of planned date (Cong, 2021).

The findings of this study demonstrated that adopting CMMI V2.0 can yield high performance results in key measures across multiple types of organizations. CMMI V2.0 can enable a proven and effective approach for performance-based improvement in software development firms. These claims are endorsed by Jii Tomiceck, CP and general manager, Honeywell, Czech Republic, who is quoted as saying, "The CMMI model taught us to think in favour of the customer and be very thorough in terms of delivering our development projects. We work to improve performance from task to task, decision to decision and project to project" (Cong, 2021, p. 5).

### Case Study: Adoption of the CMMI by Wipro Limited

This quotation is in alignment with the outcomes of the case studies at Dynanet Corporation and Wipro Limited. The process and lessons learned in these two case studies are explained by Cong (2021). Wipro Limited, the third largest company in India, was founded on December 29, 1945, by Mohamed Premji as Western India Vegetable Products Limited, later abbreviated to Wipro. It was initially set up as a manufacturer of vegetable and refined oils.

The company's value states that they are driven by their passion for quality and their commitment to customers. The company's guided philosophy is 'quality, like integrity, is simply non-negotiable'. These values and philosophies set the entire organization's standard benchmark on how each employee views quality. Essentially, quality is a critical part of Wipro's overall business strategy and plays a vital role in their results and how they approach continuous improvement. This commitment to quality and continuous improvement has positioned the company among the ten most admired companies in India.

The company has received numerous national and international awards because of its commitment to quality. These include:

- Best Managed IT Services and Best System Integrator in the CIO Choice Awards in India in 2015.
- Gold Award for Integrated Security Assurance Service under the Vulnerability Assessment, Remediation and Management category of the 11th Annual Information Security PG's Global Excellence Awards in 2015.
- Recognition as one of the world's most ethical companies by US-based Ethisphere Institute for the sixth consecutive year in 2017.
- ATD's Best of the Best Award in 2018.

In its pursuit of growth and development, during the 1970s and 1980s, the company shifted its focus to opportunities in the information technology and computing industry. Currently, it is a multinational corporation that provides IT, consulting and business process services. Its capabilities range across cloud computing, cyber security, digital transformation, artificial intelligence, robotics, data analytics and other technology consulting services in 67 countries. In 2021, its annual revenue stood at US$9.8 billion, net income at US$1.4 billion, total assets at US$11 billion and the number of employees at 231,671.

Wipro has been a pioneer in many aspects of its operation.

- It was the first company in the world to be assessed at CMMI Maturity Level 5 in 1995.
- It was one of the first IT companies to adopt Six Sigma Methodology for Continuous Improvement around 1999.
- It was one of the first companies to adopt Lean Operations for Software Development in 2005.
- It adopted the agile software development methodology around 2006.
- It adopted DevOps between 2012 and 2019.

This learning organization has three key business objectives – increasing customer satisfaction, improving operating margin and growing revenue. In an effort to meet these objectives and align with quality expectations, in 2017 the company identified several areas of focus. Having adopted CMMI practices since its inception, Wipro decided to use this model to achieve its growth objectives and selected to adopt and institutionalize the CMMI V2.0 to realize the stated objectives and make the company sustainable.

Wipro conducted a CMMI V2.0 Development view Benchmark Appraisal, targeting Maturity Level 5 with a focus on the detection of defects and increased productivity. The company aligned the Critical to Quality (CTQ) measures of CMMI V2.0 to meet their business objectives of increasing customer satisfaction, improving operating margin and growing revenue. In pursuit of these objectives, the company linked measures related to reducing defects to increasing customer satisfaction and linked measures related to productivity to improving their operating margin.

With the CMMI V2.0 intervention, Wipro was able to significantly improve Critical to Quality (CTQ) measures and business objective performance, as well as being able to identify the root causes of defects and implement processes to sustain revenues, satisfy and retain customers, increase growth and realize operating margins. In addition, throughout their continuous improvement journey, in collaboration with the CMMI V2.0, the company utilized ML and AI techniques to build predictive models based on historical project data.

In the final analysis, senior executives at Wipro believed that the company has proven that they are the pioneers in quality processes and that the CMMI journey has helped the company to develop a culture of process transformation with predictable delivery. The executives also believe that the CMMI journey has been instrumental in achieving a high level of customer satisfaction and will ensure that the company remains an industry leader in quality. Wipro's experience demonstrates that the best way to improve the external customer experience is to improve the organization internally.

### Case Study: Adoption of the CMMI by Dynanet Corporation

The case of Dynanet Corporation is another example of a company that used the CMMI V2.0 to assist them along their quality journey. Dynanet is a well-respected, solution-oriented IT organization that has over 19 years of experience in delivering world-class information technology, health technology and telecommunication solutions and services. The company was established in 1995 by Mr Sean Peay to provide IT infrastructure services to state and federal governments. Over the period, the company has moved from an IT infrastructure services company to a fully IT systems integration company. With a workforce of over 100 employees, the company has a broad professional reach, including strong partnerships with industry leaders like Booz Allen Hamilton, IBM and Leidos Lockheed Martin.

The company's mission is to provide clients with system integration services in an attempt to solve complex business problems. Based on this mission, the company seeks to create a legacy of quality, process improvement, CMMI appraisals and ISO certifications. The company passed its first ISO 9001 audit in 2009 and received the CMMI-Dev V1.2 Maturity Level 2 rating in 2009. In 2012, the company achieved the CMMI-Dev VI.3 CL3 rating, which included process areas such as project planning, project monitoring and control, requirements management, configuration management, process and product quality assurance and measurement and analysis. The company later achieved the CMMI-Dev VI.3 Maturity Level 3 rating in 2015 and 2018, and then received the CMMI-Dev V2.0 Maturity Level 5 rating in 2019. As a result of these achievements, Dynanet has been recognized as an innovative and trusted leader in the industry as they strive to deliver quick-to-market and reliable technology solutions.

In the midst of all these achievements and successes, the company was faced with a major business challenge in 2017. The company bid and won a US\$42 million software contract to enhance and maintain a large insurance system that represented 3.5% of the US GDP.

At that time the defect rate of Dynanet software deliverables began to rise and the delivery team's accuracy of effort estimates began to decline. In order to drill down to the root cause of the problems and identify the possible solutions, the company turned to the development view of the CMMI V2.0 model. It was believed that the CMMI-Dev view was a smart fit because it had practice areas for almost every aspect of Dynanet's project.

The CMMI V2.0 gave Dynanet the tools they needed to determine the root causes of their performance challenges on the project, implement the relevant corrective actions and statistically prove those actions were indeed the best solutions. With the utilization of the CMMI V2.0 dev view the company was able to achieve the following:

- a 92% decrease in the average number of high-priority defects found within 30 days after delivery of a quarterly software release;
- a 52% decrease in the rate of all software defects found from the beta testing phase through the warranty period;
- a 9% decrease in the time to resolve high-priority defects;
- a 41% decrease in the time to resolve questions about possible defects; and
- a 64% improvement in the accuracy of effort estimates.

The president and chief executive officer of the Statistical Quality Control Department at Dynanet, Kris Puthucode, is quoted as saying,

> Dynanet has seen tangible, statistically significant improvements with the continued persistence and habit of our processes that meet CMMI best practices. This is a major milestone and assures Dynanet's customers of an ongoing focus on performance excellence using the best of best practices.

The CMMI framework fed data about performance measures at the firm and project levels to senior executives in easy-to-understand formats to highlight key insights and support better decision-making. The company's long-term focus on performance improvement and its partnership with the CMMI have enhanced its quest to be a fully-data-driven company. Undoubtedly, Dynanet's CMMI Maturity Level 5 rating helped to differentiate the company from other firms in the crowded government contracting space.

### Critique of the CMMI

The CMMI was initially designed for large firms in developed economies (Iqbal et al., 2016; Niazi et al., 2010; Odeh et al., 2021). Furthermore, it is also being criticized for being cumbersome, disruptive and costly to implement even in large firms (Alsawalqah et al., 2019; Larrucea et al., 2016; Niazi et al., 2010). Consequently, the challenge to implement the CMMI is even greater in small firms which are plagued with limited resources (Staples & Niazi, 2008). Likewise, small software firms in developing economies also described CMMI-based SPI programs as time consuming, disruptive and costly to implement (Al-Ashmori et al., 2017; Espinosa-Curiel et al., 2013). The cost of model implementation, staff experience, the time needed to implement the relevant model, limited resources, intense training, document management and strict deadlines are some of the issues highlighted (Alsawalqah et al., 2019). These challenges are even greater in small software development firms in the Caribbean which have between 10 and 50 employees and an annual turnover of less than €10 million.

These constraints may limit the adoption of the CMMI by small firms (Larrucea et al., 2016).

Studies have found that small firms are not adopting and using CMMI programs, and in some cases, employees at these organizations are not knowledgeable about the CMMI (Altarawneh, 2019; Chevers & Duggan, 2007; Richardson & von Wangenheim, 2007). A study of 20 randomly selected small software development firms in developing economies in the English-speaking Caribbean (ESC) found that the majority of these firms were not using any form of SPI programs (Chevers & Duggan, 2007). This low SPI adoption rate in developing economies is due to the financial, physical and human constraints being experienced by these firms (Avgerou, 2008). These small firms are, therefore, unable to adopt the full-blown CMMI model. Yet studies have demonstrated the benefits of CMMI programs in producing high-quality software products. In response, a phased approach should be taken, which is in alignment with the continuous representation of the CMMI.

Interestingly, both large and small firms are being pressured by clients to produce high-quality software products (Herrera & Ramirez, 2003; Iqbal et al., 2016; Torrecilla-Salinasa et al., 2016). In addition, software development firms must demonstrate a high level of process maturity. It is accepted in the industry that firms must be assessed at process maturity Level 3 and above to qualify for global contracts (Niazi et al., 2010).

In an effort to increase the likelihood of small firms adopting SPI initiatives, this book presents and validates a simplified software process improvement model for small firms called SPIM-S (Chevers et al., 2017). The simplified model is in alignment with the continuous representation, less costly and easy to implement. It is derived from a set of established CMMI practices bearing in mind the constraints and norms of small software development firms in the English-speaking Caribbean. In general, small firms can be quicker, more nimble and more responsive to the dynamic software industry, usually because they have simpler organizational structures in comparison to large firms (Akman & Yilmaz, 2008). It is widely believed that the owners of small firms are often entrepreneurs who are willing to embark upon new initiatives and take the associated risks. In addition, small firms are usually more innovative than large firms, but the adoption and implementation of innovations like SPI programs may be slow, due mainly to lack of resources (Akman & Yilmaz, 2008).

### References

Akman, G., & Yilmaz, C. (2008). Innovative capability. *Innovation Strategy and Market Orientation, 12*(1), 69–111.

Al-Ashmori, A. M., Rad, B. B., & Ibrahim, S. (2017). Software process improvement frameworks as alternative of CMMI for SMEs: A literature review. *Journal of Software Engineering, 11*(2), 123–133.

Alsawalqah, H., Alshamaileh, Y., Al-Shboul, B., Shorman, A., & Sleit, A. (2019). Factors impacting on CMMI acceptance among software development firms: A quantitative assessment. *Modern Applied Science, 13*(3), 170–180.

Altarawneh, H. (2019). The impact of using CMMI practices on the success of small and medium Jordanian software firms. *Asian Journal of Information Technology, 18*(12), 250–260.

Anees, A., & Agrwal, A. (2017). Software process improvement models and their comparison. *International Journal of Advanced Research in Computer Science, 8*(5), 928–932.

Avgerou, C. (2008). Information systems in developing countries: A critical research review. *Journal of Information Technology, 23*, 133–146.

Bicego, A., & Kuvaja, P. (1996). Software process maturity and certification. *Journal of Systems Architecture, 42*(9), 611–620. Retrieved from http://portal.acm.org/citation.cfm?id=250614#.

Biro, M., & Messnarz, R. (2009). SPI experiences and innovation for global software development. *Software Process Improvement and Practice, 14*, 243–245.

Chevers, D. A., & Duggan, E. W. (2007). A modified capability framework for improving software production processes in Jamaican organizations. *The Electronic Journal on Information Systems in Developing Countries, 30*(4), 1–18.

Chevers, D. A., Mills, A. M., Duggan, E. W., & Moore, S. (2017). Towards a simplified software process improvement framework for small software development organizations. *Journal of Global Information Management, 20*(2), 110–130.

Cong, B. (2021). CMMI v2.0 performance report summary. *Information Systems Audit and Control Association*, 1–26.

Dooley, K., Subra, A., & Anderson, J. (2001). Maturity and its impact on new product development project performance. *Research in Engineering Design, 13*(1), 23–29.

Duggan, E. W., & Gibson, R. (2006). Process-centered contribution to information system quality. In E. W. Duggan & H. Reichgelt (Eds.), *Measuring information systems delivery quality* (pp. 158–180). Hershey: Ideal Group Inc.

Ebert, C., & De Man, J. (2008). Effectively utilizing project, product and process knowledge. *Information and Software Technology, 50*, 579–594.

Espinosa-Curiel, I. E., Rodriguez-Jacobo, J., & Fernandez-Zepeda, J. A. (2013). A framework for evaluation and control of the factors that influence the software process improvement in small organizations. *Journal of Software: Evolution and Process, 25*(4), 393–406.

Fiestas, I., & Sinha, S. (2011). Constraints to private investment in the poorest developing countries - A review of the literature. *Nathan*, 1–34.

Fuggetta, A. (2000). Software process: A roadmap. *Association for Computing Machinery (ACM)*, 1–9.

Gorla, N., & Lin, S. (2010). Determinants of software quality: A survey of information systems project managers. *Information and Software Technology, 52*, 602–610.

Harter, D. E., Slaughter, S. A., & Krishnan, M. S. (1998). *The life cycle effects of software quality: A longitudinal analysis.* Paper presented at the International Conference on Information Systems, Helsinki, Finland.

Hasse, V. H. (1996). Software process assessment concepts. *Journal of Systems Architecture: the EUROMICRO Journal, 42*(9), 621–631. Retrieved from http://portal.acm.org/citation.cfm?id=250602.250615.

Herrera, E. M., & Ramirez, R. A. J. (2003). A methodology for self-diagnosis for software quality assurance in small and medium-sized industries in Latin America. *The Electronic Journal on Information Systems in Developing Countries, 15*(4), 1–13.

Humphrey, W. (1989). *Managing the software process.* Reading, MA: Addison-Wesley.

Ingalsbe, J., Shoemaker, D., & Jovanovic, V. (2001). *A metamodel for the capability maturity model for software.* Paper presented at the Proceedings of the Seventh Americas Conference on Information Systems, Boston, MA, USA.

Iqbal, J., Ahmad, R. B., Nasir, M. H. N., Niazi, M., Shamshirband, S., & Asim Noor, M. A. (2016). Software SMEs' unofficial readiness for CMMI-based software process improvement. *Software Quality Journal, 24*, 997–1023.

Iversen, J., & Ngwenyama, O. (2005). Problems in measuring effectiveness in software process improvement: A longitudinal study of organizational change at Danske Data. *International Journal of Information Management, 26*, 30–43.

Khalifa, M., & Verner, J. M. (2000). Drivers for software development method usage. *IEEE Transactions on Engineering Management, 47*(3), 360–369.

Krishnan, M. S., & Keller, M. I. (1999). Measuring process consistency: Implications for reducing software defects. *IEEE Transactions on Software Engineering, 25*(6), 769–781.

Krishnan, M. S., Kriebel, C. H., Kekre, S., & Mukhopadhyay, T. (2000). An empirical analysis of productivity and quality in software products. *Management Science, 46*(6), 745–759.

Larrucea, X., O'Connor, R. V., Colomo-Palacios, R., & Laporte, C. Y. (2016). Software process improvement in very small organizations. *IEEE Software, 33*(2), 85–89.

Lee, J., Shiue, Y., & Chen, C. (2016). Examining the impacts of organizational culture and top management support of knowlede sharing on the success of software process improvement. *Computer in Human Behavior, 54*, 462–474.

Lyytinen, K. (1988). Expectation failure concept and systems analysts' view of information systems failures: Results of an exploratory study. *Information and Management, 14*(1), 45–56.

Markus, M. L., & Keil, M. (1994). If we build it they will come: Designing information systems that users want to use. *Sloan Management Review, 35*(4), 11–25.

Montoni, M. A., Rocha, A. R., & Weber, K. C. (2009). MPS.BR: A successful program for software process improvement in Brazil. *Software Process Improvement and Practice, 14*, 289–300.

Newman, M., & Robey, D. (1992). A social process model of user-analyst relationships. *MIS Quarterly, 16*(2), 249–266.

Niazi, M. (2012). An exploratory study of software process improvement implementation risks. *Journal of Software: Evolution and Process, 24*(8), 877–894.

Niazi, M., Babar, M. A., & Verner, J. M. (2010). Software process improvement barriers: A cross-cultural comparison. *Information and Software Technology, 52*(11), 1204–1216.

Odeh, A., El-Hassan, A., Abushakra, A., & Keshta, I. (2021). A model for estimating the scope of the project: A pilot study. *International Journal of Entrepreneurship, 25*(5), 1–10.

Pane, E. S., & Sarnob, R. (2015). Capability Maturity Model Integration (CMMI) for optimizing object-oriented analysis and design (OOAD). *Procedia Computer Science, 72*, 40–48.

Paulk, M. C., Curtis, B., Chrissis, M. B., & Weber, C. V. (1993). Capability Maturity Model for Software Version 1.1. *(Tech. Rep. No. CMU-eSEI-93-TR-24). Software Engineering Institute.*

Ravichandran, T., & Rai, A. (2000). Quality management in systems development: An organizational system perspective. *MIS Quarterly, 24*(3), 381–415.

Richardson, I., & von Wangenheim, C. G. (2007). Why are small software organizations different? *IEEE Software, 24*(1), 18–22.

SEI. (2005). Capability Maturity Model Integration (CMMI) version 1.1 Overview, 9. Retrieved from www.sei.cmu.eedu/cmmi/adoption/pdf/cmmi-overview05.pdf.

SEI. (2010). CMMI for Development, Version 1.3. *Carnegie Mellon University, Software Engineering Institute, CMU/SEI-2010-TR-033.*

Seliem, A., Ashour, A. S., Khalil, O. E., & Millar, S. J. (2004). Relationship of some organizational factors to information systems effectiveness: A contingency analysis of Egyptian data. *Journal of Global Information Management, 11*(1), 40–71.

Serrano, M. A., Montes de Oca, C., & Cedillo, K. (2006, October 19–20). *An experience on implementing the CMMI in a small organization using the team software process.* Paper presented at the First International Research Workshop for Process Improvement in Small Settings, Pittsburgh, Carnegie Mellon University.

Standish Group, T. (2015). Standish group 2015 Chaos report. *The Standish Group*, 1–16.

Staples, M., & Niazi, M. (2008). Systematic review of organizational motivations for adopting CMM-based SPI. *Information and Software Technology, 50*, 605–620.

Sulayman, M., Urquhart, C., Mendes, E., & Seidel, S. (2012). Software process improvement success factors for small and medium Web companies: A qualitative study. *Information and Software Technology, 54*(5), 479–500.

Torrecilla-Salinasa, C. J., Sedeñoa, J., Escalonaa, M. J., & Mejíasa, M. (2016). Agile,Web Engineering and Capability Maturity Model Integration: Asystematic literature review. *Information and Software Technology, 71,* 92–107.

Vasconcellos, F. J. S., Landre, G. B., Cunha, J. O. G., Oliveira, J. L., Ferreira, R., & Vincenzi, A. M. R. (2017). Approaches to strategic alignment of software process improvement: A systematic literature review *The Journal of System and Software, 123,* 45–63.

# 5

# THE SIMPLIFIED SOFTWARE PROCESS IMPROVEMENT MODEL FOR SMALL FIRMS

Software quality is viewed as a strategic issue because it provides a competitive advantage. Software products are fundamentally different from other types of products because they are intangible, evolve quickly and have no physical form (Altarawneh, 2019). To increase the likelihood of developing and delivering a high-quality software product, a good and relevant process improvement model should be applied. However, it is felt that the popular and well-established CMMI framework is intended for large firms in developed economies with large projects having huge budgets (Altarawneh, 2019; Iqbal et al., 2016; Niazi et al., 2010; Odeh et al., 2021). In accordance with this view, this book seeks to tailor/customize the CMMI to override various operational constraints in small software development firms.

A mixed methods approach was taken to customize the CMMI to develop a simplified software process improvement model for small firms called SPIM-S. A mixed methods research design is a procedure for collecting, analysing and mixing both qualitative and quantitative research and methods in a single study to understand the research problem (Creswell, 2009). A mixed methods approach was chosen because both qualitative and quantitative data, together, provide a better understanding of this research problem than either type by itself. An exploratory, sequential, mixed methods design was used in this study. This is characterized by an initial qualitative phase of data collection and analysis, followed by a phase of quantitative data collection and analysis, with a final phase of integration or the linking of data from the two separate streams of data (Creswell, 2009).

The objective of the first phase was to derive a set of CMMI Levels 2 and 3 process practices that are relevant and applicable to small software development firms in developing economies based on their norms, culture and constraints. With these in mind the research question for the qualitative phase was, "What are the relevant and applicable CMMI process activities for small software development firms in developing economies?" The objective of the second phase was to validate the derived list of CMMI Levels 2 and 3 process practices (called the proposed simplified process improvement model for small firms – SPIM-S). The research question in this quantitative phase was, "What is the impact of people, process and technology in determining the quality of the software product for small firms in developing economies?"

### Phase 1 – The Qualitative Method

A series of focus group sessions utilizing a group technique called the nominal group technique (NGT) was used in this phase. Firstly, the NGT was chosen because it contributes to greater objectivity as it seeks to reduce emotional attachment to ideas by hiding the source of each generated idea, while increasing the likelihood of maximizing participation in and contribution to the results (Delbecq & Van de Ven, 1971); (Zuech, 1992). In essence, the technique minimizes negative group behaviours that inhibit the free flow of information and opinions. In freely interacting groups, these negative behaviours include (1) conforming behaviour, (2) anchoring, (3) groupthink and (4) the Abilene Paradox. *Conforming* behaviour refers to a lack of significant deviation from the average, expected behaviour or norm, while *anchoring* is a common human tendency to rely too heavily on one piece of information when making decisions. *Groupthink* is a type of thought exhibited by group members who try to minimize conflict and reach a consensus without critically testing, analysing and evaluating ideas. Finally, the *Abilene Paradox* is a situation in which a group of people collectively decide on a course of action that is counter to the preferences of any of the individuals in the group.

The NGT, in contrast, promotes a silent and confidential approach to idea generation which enhances creative thinking and by extension can lead to a rich discussion with the likelihood of having a better solution to the problem (Delbecq et al., 1986; Moore, 1987). The approach taken was as follows.

1. Idea Selection
   (a) Participants were given a list of all established 18 CMMI Levels 2 and 3 process practices.
   (b) On 3" × 5" cards participants were asked to silently (i) select or merge any of the 18 CMMI practices or (ii) add in 'new' practices, deemed relevant and applicable within the context of the English-speaking Caribbean.
2. Round-robin of ideas
   (a) Cards were collected by the independent facilitator, shuffled and randomly returned to participants.
   (b) Participants were asked to verbally state one idea per card in a round-robin manner (the purpose of shuffling the cards was to hide the identity of the generator of each idea).
3. Clarification of ideas
   (a) Participants were asked to explain the meaning of new or merged practices. It was not required to defend or provide a detailed justification for the merger.
   (b) Duplicates (practices) were eliminated.
4. Select the top ten practices
   (a) Participants were asked to select the top ten practices.
   (b) These were recorded and tallied.
   (c) The ten most frequent practices were selected.
5. Ranking
   (a) Participants were asked to silently rank these ten practices, with the most important practices being given a score of 10 and the least a score of 1.
   (b) The scores were recorded and tallied.
6. Decision-making

   (a) The practice with the highest score was ranked as number 1, the next highest score as number 2, etc.
   (b) The final list was presented to the group for their comment and approval.

Secondly, three pilot sessions were held in Jamaica using the NGT approach to identify the relevant and applicable CMMI Levels 2 and 3 process practices based on the norms, culture and constraints in Jamaica. The participants in these three pilot sessions were graduate students at the University of the West Indies, Mona, pursuing their PhD in Information Systems and lecturers at the University of the West Indies, Mona, who have been teaching the Master of Science in Computer-based Management Information Systems. Both students and lecturers have been involved in software development projects.

Thirdly, four real focus group sessions were held in four English-speaking Caribbean countries, namely, Barbados, Guyana, Jamaica, and Trinidad and Tobago. The participants in these sessions were software developers and project managers. Thirty persons participated in the four sessions. The NGT sessions, on average, lasted for two hours and were managed by an independent facilitator, not the researcher. Participants were asked to identify relevant and applicable software development practices which they considered important, based on the norms and constraints in their respective countries. They were also given instructions to merge any process areas that they felt were necessary based on their knowledge and experience.

Upon completion of the four focus group sessions, 24 practices were identified and ranked. The total of 24 practices was higher than the original 18 established CMMI Levels 2 and 3 practices, because a few practices were combined and new practices introduced. This increase supports the notion that the NGT process can facilitate the generation of creative ideas. Subsequent to the four sessions in which participants ranked the top 12 practices, scores were assigned in descending order from 12 to 1. Table 5.1 outlines the 12 top-ranked practices in each country. For example, Risk Management (RSKM) was ranked as number one in Guyana, followed by Project Planning (PP), then Requirement Development (RD), and so these were given scores of 12, 11 and 10, respectively. Likewise, for Jamaica and Trinidad and Tobago the top-ranked practice was Requirements Development merged with Requirements Management (RD + RM). Based on the approach taken, this practice was given a score of 12 in Jamaica and Trinidad and Tobago. The same approach was taken regarding Barbados where the top-ranked practice was Requirement Management merged with Organization Process Definition (RM + OPD) which was given a score of 12.

Upon the completion of the ranking of the practices, tallying was done to ascertain the highly ranked practices in the four countries. For example, Risk Management (RSKM) received scores of 12, 9,

**Table 5.1**   Top Ranked Practices in Each Country

| GUYANA | | JAMAICA | | TRINIDAD | | BARBADOS | |
|---|---|---|---|---|---|---|---|
| RSKM | 12 | RD+RM | 12 | RD+RM | 12 | RM+OPD | 12 |
| PP | 11 | IPM+PP+PMC | 11 | TS | 11 | RSKM | 11 |
| RD | 10 | OT | 10 | IPM | 10 | OT | 10 |
| TS | 9 | RSKM | 9 | RSKM | 9 | PP+PMC | 9 |
| IPM | 8 | TS | 8 | VER+VAL | 8 | TS | 8 |
| PMC | 7 | OPD | 7 | OT | 7 | OPF | 7 |
| OT | 6 | OPF | 6 | PMC | 6 | RD | 6 |
| VER+VAL | 5 | PI+VER+VAL | 5 | PP | 5 | OPD | 5 |
| OPD | 4 | PPQA | 4 | OPF | 4 | IPM | 4 |
| VER | 3 | VER | 3 | OPD | 3 | PP | 3 |
| OPF | 2 | M&A | 2 | CM | 2 | RM | 2 |
| VAL | 1 | PI+VAL | 1 | PI | 1 | DAR | 1 |

**Table 5.2**   The Top Ranked Practices in Descending Order

| NO. | PRACTICES | SCORE | CMMI MATURITY LEVEL |
|---|---|---|---|
| 1 | RSKM | 41 | 3 |
| 2 | TS | 36 | 3 |
| 3 | OT | 33 | 3 |
| 4 | RD+RM | 24 | 2 & 3 |
| 5 | IPM | 22 | 3 |
| 6 | PP | 19 | 2 |
| 7 | OPD | 19 | 3 |
| 8 | OPF | 19 | 3 |
| 9 | PMC | 13 | 2 |
| 10 | VER+VAL | 13 | 3 |

11 and 9 in Guyana, Jamaica, Trinidad and Tobago, and Barbados, respectively, resulting in a grand total of 41. The practice with the next highest score was Technical Solution (TS), receiving a grand total of 36. Table 5.2 outlines the top 10 practices with their associated scores and their established CMMI maturity levels. The tallying process yielded a list of 10 highly ranked practices (the 'Top Ten') for small software development firms in developing economies.

Table 5.3 presents the resulting simplified framework of the top ten ranked CMMI practices with their scores, designations and assigned maturity levels. The original CMMI framework had 18 practices in Levels 2 and 3. However, the resultant framework was

**Table 5.3**    The Software Process Improvement Model for Small Firms (SPIM-S)

| RANK | PRACTICES | SCORE | DESIGNATION | ASSIGNED MATURITY LEVEL |
|------|-----------|-------|-------------|-------------------------|
| 1 | RSKM | 41 | Risk Management | 3 |
| 2 | TS | 36 | Technical Solution | 3 |
| 3 | OT | 33 | Organization Training | 3 |
| 4 | RD+RM | 24 | Requirements Development and Requirements Management | 2 |
| 5 | IPM | 22 | Integrated Project Management | 3 |
| 6 | PP | 19 | Project Planning | 2 |
| 7 | OPD | 19 | Organization Process Definition | 3 |
| 8 | OPF | 19 | Organization Process Focus | 3 |
| 9 | PMC | 13 | Project Monitoring and Control | 2 |
| 10 | VER+VAL | 13 | Verification and Validation | 3 |

more simplified converging on only ten practices – three assigned to Level 2 and seven assigned to Level 3. The assigned levels were guided by the CMMI approach in which Level 2 practices deal with project management activities and Level 3 practices are concerned with organization-wide process management activities. This constitutes the software process improvement model for small firms (SPIM-S), as shown in Table 5.3.

The result of this study yielded a more simplified software process improvement model, with a 45% reduction (from 18 to 10) in the number of process practices in comparison with the original CMMI model. The proposed simplified model has no practices at Level 1 which is consistent with the original CMMI model. Because a phased approach is being taken to develop this model, there are currently no practices at Levels 4 and 5. In time, it is expected that firms will gradually incorporate some advanced practices at Levels 4 and 5 when learning and institutionalization of the current practices have taken place.

In examining the top three highly ranked practices (which are all Level 3 practices) – risk management, technical solution and organization training, it is evident that software developers and project managers in the Caribbean are generally more concerned with organization-wide process management factors. These include the identification of all possible risks in an effort to overcome project exposures, finding the best solution that meets users' requirements and equipping the project team members with the necessary knowledge so that they can execute their tasks in the most efficient manner. This claim is made based on the aims of these practices as defined by the Software Engineering Institute. The aims are:

1. Risk management – to identify potential problems before they occur so that risk-handling activities can be planned and invoked as needed across the life of the product or project to mitigate adverse impacts on achieving objectives;
2. Technical solution – to design, develop and implement solutions to requirements; and
3. Organization training – to develop the skills and knowledge of people so that they can perform their roles effectively and efficiently.

The top three practices of risk management, technical solution and organization training may reflect the desire of these firms to take the necessary precaution, design the optimal solution and engage in capacity building in light of the limited resources in finance, people skills, equipment and material in the Caribbean region.

The goal is for small software development firms in this region to seek to increase the capabilities of these top ten practices by taking them to the stage of institutionalization. Upon reaching this stage, effort should be made to institutionalize the other Levels 2 and 3 practices like measurement and analysis, configuration management, decision analysis and resolution and product integration. At a later date, the Levels 4 and 5 practices like organizational process performance and causal analysis and resolution could be adopted and institutionalized. This phased approach would gradually increase the competitiveness of these small firms, thus increasing the likelihood of winning global contracts.

### Phase 2 – The Quantitative Method

The key objective of the quantitative phase was to validate the proposed SPIM-S framework. A survey using a matched-pair design was used to validate the SPIM-S framework. The impact of the top 10 ranked process practices alongside technology and people on software

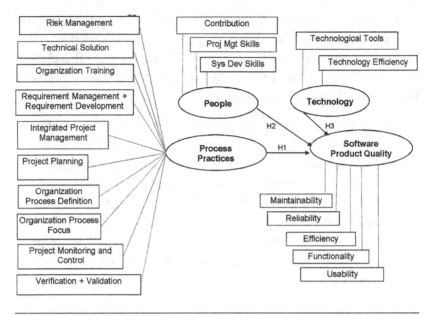

**Figure 5.1**   The research model.

quality was assessed. Figure 5.1 shows the research model along with the associated hypotheses. Based on the literature, the three hypotheses are:

- H1: The institutionalization of process practices will have a positive impact on software product quality.
- H2: People skills will have a positive impact on software product quality.
- H3: The use of technological tools will have a positive impact on software product quality.

The targeted organizations were small software development firms based on the European Commission. The unit of analysis was software development projects in Barbados, Guyana, Jamaica, and Trinidad and Tobago that develop software products for sale or in-house use. The sample frame was developed by the researcher using phone lists, referrals and other contacts. Contacts via phone calls or emails were made with the chief executive officer, chief information officer or owners of the firms regarding the purpose of the study, who then referred the researcher to software developers/project managers of recently completed software development projects. Recently completed projects were those projects that were completed within the last two years. The survey instrument was distributed online to the relevant software developer/project manager with the responsibility for the project. Each software developer/project manager was asked to complete a set of questions related to process practices, technology and the people aspects of their respective project. The software developer/project managers were then asked to forward the survey instrument to a key user who would be required to respond to questions related to the quality of the delivered software product. Altogether, there were 112 developer/user dyads who completed the survey. The justification to take the developer/user dyad approach was based on the notion that while software developers might evaluate a software project as a success, other groups like users and top management might attribute it as a failure (Dwivedi et al., 2014).

### Survey Instrument Development

All constructs were operationalized as multidimensional with each sub-dimension consisting of multiple items (2–4 items each). Appendix B provides further details on the survey items. Responses were captured using 7-point Likert-type scales anchored as (1) Strongly Disagree and (7) Strongly Agree. In cases where practices were not in place, respondents were asked to indicate 'not applicable' and these instances were coded as 0.

The software process consisted of ten sub-dimensions (process practices) and was measured using items from the CMMI 'Maturity Questionnaire' (Zubrow et al., 1994). Software quality was assessed in terms of five dimensions, namely maintainability, functionality, usability, efficiency and reliability, and multi-item scales (with 2–3 items each) adapted from Lewis (1995). The survey items for the people and technology constructs were newly developed.

The survey instrument was pilot tested using 17 information systems researchers, research methods specialists and graduate information systems students in Jamaica and Trinidad and Tobago. Feedback was provided and the relevant adjustments made. Some of the adjustments included the time needed to complete the survey, changes to ambiguous questions and changes to compound questions.

## Data Collection

The survey instrument was distributed online to the targeted organizations in Jamaica, Barbados, Guyana and Trinidad and Tobago. The software developer/project manager represented someone who was knowledgeable about the practices and resources used to plan, organize, schedule and deploy the respective software product and could evaluate the project from an internal perspective. The user respondent represented someone who could provide a separate evaluation of the quality of the software product from an external perspective. The survey instrument had two parts. Part A listed questions related to the process practices, people and technology and were answered by the software developer/project manager, while Part B on the quality of the software product was completed by a user-respondent of the same software project.

A total of 360 survey links were distributed via email to small software development firms; 136 responses were returned, but 24 were incomplete. This resulted in a response rate of 31% (n = 112). The profiles of the respondents are set out below. The majority of the respondents came from Jamaica (63%), followed by Trinidad and Tobago (21%). This was expected as these two countries are by far the largest of the four countries, in terms of population and number of software development firms. Several sectors were represented, with responses coming from information technology (26%), government (18%), education (11%) and communications (10%). The average project complexity was just above mid-range at 4.8 (on a scale of 1–7). Software developer/project manager experience ranged from one to 30 years (mean = 9.1 years, SD = 7.3). Most of the project teams were small, where 9% had less than three members, 32% had three to five members, 26% had 6–10 members, and 13% and 20% had 11–15 and >15 members, respectively.

## Data Analysis

Partial least squares (PLS) was used to test the research model because of its ability to handle relatively small sample sizes, and model formative and reflective constructs (Chin, 2010). PLS Graph 3.0 was used to assess the measurement and structural models. Bootstrap re-sampling (500 re-samples) was used to determine the significance of the paths within the structural model.

The composite reliability measures ranged from 0.816 to 0.977 (as shown in Table 5.4). This meant that reliability was established in all the survey items as the composite reliability readings were above the recommended threshold of 0.70 (Chin, 2010). The results also show AVE values ranging from 0.553 to 0.933. These values are above the recommended threshold of 0.50, suggesting adequate validity among the constructs (Chin, 2010).

The descriptive statistics for the process practices, technology, people and software product quality constructs are reported in Table 5.4. The results show the firms evaluated their software product quality at just above the mid-point (on the 1–7 scale), with usability being the

**Table 5.4** Descriptive Statistics and Reliabilities

| VARIABLE (# OF ITEMS) | DESCRIPTION | MEAN | SD | COMPOSITE RELIABILITY (CR) | AVERAGE VARIANCE EXTRACTED (AVE) |
|---|---|---|---|---|---|
| SOFTWARE PROCESS | | | | | |
| RSKM (4) | Risk Management | 4.43 | 1.738 | 0.949 | 0.823 |
| TS (3) | Technical Solution | 4.81 | 1.298 | 0.836 | 0.630 |
| OT (3) | Organization Training | 4.80 | 1.599 | 0.886 | 0.722 |
| RMRD (4) | Requirement Management + Requirement Development | 4.89 | 1.247 | 0.837 | 0.570 |
| IPM (3) | Integrated Project Management | 4.52 | 1.687 | 0.894 | 0.737 |
| PP (5) | Project Planning | 4.88 | 1.309 | 0.869 | 0.573 |
| OPD (3) | Organization Process Definition | 4.23 | 1.968 | 0.951 | 0.867 |
| OPF (3) | Organization Process Focus | 4.02 | 1.816 | 0.921 | 0.797 |
| PMC (4) | Project Monitoring and Control | 4.71 | 1.338 | 0.848 | 0.589 |
| VV (4) | Verification + Validation | 4.76 | 1.514 | 0.941 | 0.800 |
| PEOPLE | | | | | |
| CONTR (3) | Quality of Contribution to Project | 5.46 | 1.237 | 0.879 | 0.708 |
| PMSKL (4) | Project Management Skills | 4.98 | 1.252 | 0.830 | 0.553 |
| SDSKL (3) | Systems Development Skills | 5.07 | 1.575 | 0.863 | 0.677 |
| TECHNOLOGY | | | | | |
| TTOOL (2) | Technological Tools | 2.89 | 2.048 | 0.816 | 0.690 |
| TEFFI (2) | Technology Efficiency | 3.13 | 2.150 | 0.954 | 0.913 |
| IS QUALITY | | | | | |
| MAINT (3) | Maintainability | 3.96 | 1.724 | 0.913 | 0.778 |
| RELIAB (3) | Reliability | 4.61 | 1.793 | 0.884 | 0.718 |
| EFFICI (2) | Efficiency | 4.76 | 1.662 | 0.925 | 0.860 |
| FUNCT (3) | Functionality | 4.92 | 1.645 | 0.913 | 0.779 |
| USABIL (3) | Usability | 5.06 | 1.607 | 0.977 | 0.933 |

highest-ranked dimension (mean = 5.06, SD = 1.61) and maintainability the lowest ranked (mean = 3.96, SD = 1.72). On average, all firms had some software process practices in place, with the mean response being around the mid-range (mean = 4.60, SD = 1.55). This suggests that the top 10 ranked process practices were established but not institutionalized.

At the same time, the firms appeared to have reasonable access to people-related skills (e.g. project management and software development skills) with those involved making significant contributions to the success of the project (mean = 5.17, SD = 1.35). The results also showed that technology aspects were evaluated on average as below the mid-point (mean = 3.01, SD = 2.10). The standard deviation for the technology construct was the highest (2.10 versus 1.61, 1.55 and 1.35), suggesting that the use of technological tools had the highest variation in comparison to process practices and people.

### Structural Model

Figure 5.2 shows the results of the research model. The $R^2$ of 0.276 indicates that software process practices, technology and people explained 0.276 of the variance in software product quality. This means that there are factors other than process practices, technology and people that can influence software product quality. These

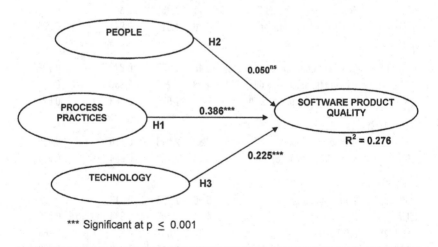

*** Significant at $p \leq 0.001$

**Figure 5.2**   Results of the research model.

could be culture, project size, team size or the complexity of the projects. These other factors could explain 72.4% of the variance in software product quality. The results also indicate a positive relationship between process practices ($\beta$ = 0.386, p ≤ 0.01) and technology ($\beta$ = 0.225, p ≤ 0.01) on software product quality. Thus, supporting hypotheses $H_1$ and $H_3$, respectively. This finding is consistent with prior research (Dooley et al., 2001; Iversen & Ngwenyama, 2006). However, contrary to expectations, the people element was not significant regarding software product quality. Thus, hypothesis $H_2$ was not supported.

### Discussion and Implications

The purpose of this book was to propose and evaluate a simplified software process improvement model for small firms (SPIM-S). This was done by examining the impact of the process practices, people and technology on software product quality. Using data from small software development firms in the Caribbean, the tests of the simplified SPIM-S confirmed the expectation that the software process practices and technology have a positive impact on software quality. The model collectively explained 27.6% of the variance observed for software quality, with process practices having the greater impact. The results were consistent with prior research which have explained 21–32% of the variance observed for software product quality

The study also made an assessment of the current state of small firms in the Caribbean with respect to the top-ranked process practices. The study confirmed that most software development firms in the Caribbean are, in general, operating at Level 2 or Level 3 in terms of process maturity. While process practices had the greatest impact on software quality, only three out of ten practices were significant at the 90% level. These were organization process definition, organization process focus and, verification and validation, that are all Level 3 practices. A probable explanation for why these three practices were significant could be the emphasis that small firms place on the importance of project activities like reviews, inspections and quality assurance during software development

In addition, it could be deduced that the other seven practices may not have been well-embedded in the software development process and, as a result, had no significant impact on the quality of the software product delivered. This might be so because the majority of software development firms in the Caribbean are not fully aware of the benefits of SPI programs and, hence, are not using SPI initiatives to support their software development and delivery process. Due to the limited development processes practices, these firms might have a long way to go in improving their software development processes and complying with international quality standards. It is imperative that top executive, software developers and project managers in small software development firms in the Caribbean attend training seminars and workshops on SPI and the CMMI in an effort to increase the maturity of their software developmental process.

**Appendix A: Definitions of SPI Terms**

1. **Requirements Management and Requirements Development** are about analysing and producing the system requirements and managing customer requirements.
2. **Project Planning** establishes and maintains the plans that define project activities.
3. **Verification** describes the steps taken to ensure that the activities are performed in compliance with processes such as reviews, audits and software quality assurance while **Validation** is checking that the software process produced the intended results such as formal walkthroughs and inspections.
4. **Project Monitoring and Control** provides an understanding of the project's progress so that appropriate corrective actions can be taken when the project's performance deviates significantly from the plan.
5. **Technical Solution** is about designing, developing and implementing solutions to user requirements.
6. **Organization Process Definition** establishes and maintains a usable set of software development procedures and standards.
7. **Organization Process Focus** plans, implements and deploys process improvements based on a thorough understanding of the strengths and weaknesses of the organization's software development processes.

8. **Organization Training** is about developing the skills and knowledge of project personnel so they can perform their roles effectively and efficiently.

9. **Integrated Project Management** is about managing the project in a manner that brings team members together in a coordinated manner.

10. **Risk Management** is about identifying potential problems before they occur so that risk-management activities can be planned and put into action as needed.

Source: (SEI, 2010; Zubrow et al., 1994)

**Appendix B: The Survey Items**

**Software Process Improvement Practices**

*Requirements Management and Requirements Development*

RMRD01. Requirements were well established for this project

RMRD02. Detailed records were kept of the requirement changes in this project

RMRD03. Requirement management and requirement development on this project were guided by organization policy

RMRD04. Performance measures (e.g. total number of requirements changes that were proposed, opened, approved or closed) were in place on this project for requirement management and requirement development

*Project Planning*

PP01. Detailed cost estimates were in place for managing this project

PP02. Detailed time estimates were in place for managing this project

PP03. All relevant tasks were identified for the successful execution of this project

PP04. Adequate resources were in place for the planning of this project (e.g. funding, expertise, etc.)

PP05. Performance measures (e.g. completion of milestones) were in place for planning this project

*Project Monitoring and Control*

PM01. Corrective actions were always taken to manage variances (actual vs plan) in this project

PM02. Changes to development plans were always signed off by relevant stakeholders in this project

PM03. Organization policies were in place for guiding project monitoring and control in this project

PM04. Performance measures were in place to assess project monitoring and control in this project

*Technical Solution*

TS01. A well-established plan was developed to address all requirements for this project

TS02. All needed resources were in place to execute the solution for all the requirements in this project

TS03. Performance measures were in place to assess the effectiveness of technical solutions for this project

*Verification and Validation*

VV01. Verification activities were effectively planned for this project

VV02. Validation activities were effectively planned for this project

VV03. Adequate resources were provided to perform verification activities in this project

VV04. Adequate resources were provided to perform validation activities in this project

*Organization Process Definition*

OPD01. The organization's software development processes were adequately documented in this project

OPD02. The organization's software development processes were clearly understood in this project

OPD03. Performance measures were in place to assess if key stakeholders understand the firm's software development processes and procedures covered by this project

*Organization Process Focus*

OPF01. There were established software development processes to be followed by key stakeholders in this project

OPF02. Adequate measures were taken to adjust the organization's software development processes based on performance indicators for this project

OPF03. Performance measures were in place to assess the effectiveness of all organization software development processes in this project

*Organization Training*

OT01. Project team members were adequately trained to perform their roles in this project

OT02. Adequate resources were provided to facilitate training for this project

OT03. Performance measures were in place to assess the effectiveness of training in this project

*Integrated Project Management*

IPM01. A well-established policy document regarding the integration of all relevant project team members was in place for this project

IPM02. High levels of co-operation were encouraged among all relevant project groups in this project

IPM03. Performance measures were in place to assess the integration of project team members in this project

*Risk Management*

RSKM01. Potential risks were clearly identified for this project

RSKM02. A clearly defined action plan was established for possible risks in this project

RSKM03. All needed resources were in place to address potential risks in this project

RSKM04. Performance measures were in place to assess the management of risk in this project

**People Skills**

*Project Management Skills*

PMSK01. High levels of project management skills (e.g. project estimating, planning, controlling) were displayed on this project

PMSK02. High levels of process expertise were available during the execution of this project

PMSK03. High levels of system analysis and design expertise were available during the execution of this project

PMSK04. Adequate understanding of modelling techniques was displayed during the execution of this project

*Systems Development Skills*

SDSK01. Competent data analysts and database administrators were assigned to this project

SDSK02. Competent systems construction personnel were assigned to this project (e.g. programmers, networkers, etc.)

SDSK03. Competent code testers and documentation personnel were assigned to this project

*Contribution*

CONT01. Project members contributed greatly to the success of this project

CONT02. Project members participated equally in the execution of the project

CONT03. Project members contributed to the project achieving its stated objectives

**Technological Tools**

*Technology Tools*

TTOOL01. Project management software (e.g. Microsoft Project, Primavera, Timeline, Rational, or others) was used in the execution of this project

TTOOL02. Computer aided software engineering (CASE) systems were used in the execution of this project

*Technology Effectiveness*

> TTEFFI3. Using technological tools (such as project manage-
> ment software, modelling technologies, CASE tools, etc.)
> increased the efficiency of this project
>
> TTEFFI4. Using technological tools (such as project manage-
> ment software, modelling technologies, CASE tools, etc.)
> increased the effectiveness of this project

## Software Quality

*Functionality*

> FUNCT01. The delivered system features are suitable for
> achieving the business objectives
>
> FUNCT02. The system generally provides the support I need
> to do my job
>
> FUNCT03. I am not tempted to work around the system to
> perform system tasks

*Reliability*

> RELIAB01. The delivered system is usually available when
> needed
>
> RELIAB02. I can easily recover from input errors
>
> RELIAB03. The system is usually restored quickly after a failure

*Usability*

> USABIL01. The delivered system is easy to understand
>
> USABIL02. The delivered system is easy to learn
>
> USABIL03. The delivered system is easy to use

*Efficiency*

> EFFIC01. The response time of the system is generally acceptable
>
> EFFIC02. It is generally easy to invoke systems features

*Maintainability*

MAINT01. The delivered system provides diagnostics that help to identify causes of failures

MAINT02. Relatively little effort is expended to correct faults whenever system errors occur

MAINT03. Relatively little effort is needed to test system modifications

## References

Altarawneh, H. (2019). The impact of using CMMI practices on the success of small and medium Jordanian software firms. *Asian Journal of Information Technology, 18*(12), 250–260.

Chin, W. W. (2010). *How to write-up and report PLS analysis.* Berlin Heidelberg: Springer - Verlag.

Creswell, J. W. (2009). *Research design: Qualitative, quantitative, and mixed methods approaches* (3rd ed.). Los Angeles: SAGE.

Delbecq, A. L., & Van de Ven, A. H. (1971). A group process model for problem identification and program planning. *Applied Behavioural Science, 7,* 466–491.

Delbecq, A. L., Van de Ven, A. H., & Gustafson, D. H. (1986). *Group techniques for program planning: A guide to nominal group and delphi processes.* Middleton, WI: Greenbriar.

Dooley, K., Subra, A., & Anderson, J. (2001). Maturity and its impact on new product development project performance. *Research in Engineering Design, 13*(1), 23–29.

Dwivedi, Y. K., Wastell, D., Laumer, S., Henriksen, H. Z., Myers, M. D., Bunker, D., Elbanna, A., Ravishankar, M. N., & Srivastava, S. (2014). Research on information systems failures and success: Status update and future directions. *Information System Frontier, 17*(1), 143–157.

Iqbal, J., Ahmad, R. B., Nasir, M. H. N., Niazi, M., Shamshirband, S., & Asim Noor, M. A. (2016). Software SMEs' unofficial readiness for CMMI_-based software process improvement. *Software Quality Journal, 24,* 997–1023.

Iversen, J., & Ngwenyama, O. (2006). Problems in measuring effectiveness in software process improvement: A longitudinal study of organizational change at Danske Data. *International Journal of Information Management, 26*(1), 30–43.

Lewis, J. R. (1995). IBM computer usability satisfaction questionnaire: Psychometric evaluation and instructions for use. *International Journal of Human-Computer Interaction, 7*(1), 57–78.

Moore, C. M. (1987). *Group techniques for idea building.* Newbury Park, CA: Sage.

Niazi, M., Babar, M. A., & Verner, J. M. (2010). Software process improvement barriers: A cross-cultural comparison. *Information and Software Technology*, *52*(11), 1204–1216.

Odeh, A., El-Hassan, A., Abushakra, A., & Keshta, I. (2021). A model for estimating the scope of the project: A pilot study. *International Journal of Entrepreneurship*, *25*(5), 1–10.

SEI. (2010). CMMI for Development, Version 1.3. *Carnegie Mellon University, Software Engineering Institute, CMU/SEI-2010-TR-033*.

Zubrow, D., Hayes, W., Siegel, J., & Goldenson, D. (1994). Maturity Questionnaire, 7. Retrieved from www.sei.cmu.edu/publications/documents/94.reports/94.sr.007.html. Accessed on January 5, 2006.

Zuech, N. (1992). Identifying and ranking opportunities for machine vision in a facility. *Industrial Engineering*, *24*, 42–44.

# 6

## CONCLUSION

Software development has become a difficult and challenging, yet important, activity in the modern world (Shaikh & Abro, 2019). Efficient software development is essential for both organizations and individuals, but it requires detailed planning, organizing, monitoring and testing in order to deliver high-quality software products (Akinsanya et al., 2019). In 2020, the total cost of poor software quality in the US was estimated at US$2.08 trillion (Krasner, 2021). The incidence of technical coding errors with the Boeing 737 flight in 2018 and the incidence of the software defect of the A400M aircraft in 2015 are examples of poor software quality. These and other software failures can be costly, devastating and, sometimes, lead to loss of lives.

This book is intended to provide sufficient information to stimulate further discussion on the best developmental approach to deliver high-quality software products and successful software projects. The difficulty being experienced by software development firms is even more pronounced in small firms in developing economies (Chevers et al., 2020; Heeks, 2002).

The debate has started and continues regarding the best production method to be used based on available resources and the context of the developmental environment. Should the waterfall, user-centred, reuse-based or incremental methods be employed, or should a hybrid approach be taken? These are some of the critical decisions to be made in software development. Such decisions can determine the success or failure of software projects and, by extension, the sustainability of software development firms.

In 2001, 17 software developers met to discuss better ways of developing software products. In their deliberation, it was agreed to value some core principles in software development. The net result of those deliberations led to the 'Agile Manifesto' which embodies the guiding tenets of the agile methods. The core principles include:

- individuals and interactions over process and tools;
- working software over comprehensive documentation;
- customer collaboration over contract negotiation; and
- responding to change over following a plan.

On another occasion, a panel session was held by the Working Group of the International Federation for Information Processing (IFIP) in Bangalore in 2013. The aim of these discussions was to reflect on the need for new research perspectives and guidance for key stakeholders on the factors that enhance software project success and techniques to avoid failures (Dwivedi et al., 2014). It was decided that the phenomena of project success and/or failure should be studied from multiple perspectives.

It is widely agreed that the capability and contribution of people, the development tools used and the established developmental process that is followed are key factors for the success or failure of any software project (Caldeira et al., 2019). In other words, the lack of synergy between social and technical factors can be a hindrance to project success (Mens et al., 2019). This synergistic blend has become even more relevant today with the proliferation of open-source software development and distributed teams. The need for coordination and collaboration has led to a concept known as 'social coding' in which team members rely on integrated platforms and collaborative tools (development tools) to enhance effective communication, interaction and coordination. This is supported by the claim that team capability and customer involvement are the main factors contributing to the success of software development projects (Tam et al., 2020).

In addition, cultural diversity, geographic dispersion and project size have created further complexity to an already complex process, thus requiring greater social skills by software developers, project managers and users. These recent trends have created the need for future research to evaluate their influence or non-influence on the ISO/IEC quality characteristics of functionality, reliability, usability, efficiency, maintainability and portability in various contexts. That is, what is the impact of cultural diversity, geographic location and project size on software product quality? In these studies, the ISO/IEC quality characteristics would be the dependent variable. The attainment of these quality characteristics is critical, more so because they can provide a competitive advantage (Porter, 1985).

## Software Production Methods

One of the greatest challenges in software projects is to devise a plan of action to avoid failures. It is evident that in the series of software production methods, it is an effort to develop and deliver high-quality software products which, by extension, can lead to successful projects. Software products are essentially a picture of human ideas. Hence, the delivered software product is a representation of thoughts presented in binary codes and not a physical object. That is why different production methods (from the waterfall model to incremental methods to hybrid methods) are required to produce these intangible software products based on various contexts (Dwivedi et al., 2012; Shaikh & Abro, 2019).

It is important to note that 'one size does not fit all'. Software developers and project managers must be cognisant regarding which levels (production methods) to pull, in which context and at what time. It is suggested that a 'silver pellet' approach should be taken to chip away at the danger of producing poor quality software products, rather than a 'silver bullet' approach (Duggan, 2006). For example, large projects can be broken down into small projects and an agile approach taken if the software product will not be used in a critical-sensitive industry. It is strongly recommended that agile methods should be used in the following contexts.

- small-scale software products;
- the project team is small and can co-locate;
- solving unstructured problems;
- requirements are dynamic;
- difficult for users to specify the requirements of the software product;
- the software product will not put people and critical organizations at risk.

The proposal in 2020 to introduce 'scrumbanfall' is an example of a hybrid approach to software development. Scrumbanfall is the agile hybridization of scrum and kanban with a waterfall approach in software development (Bhavsar et al., 2020). Both scrum and kanban are members of the agile family that are extensively used in software development. By themselves, both scrum and kanban have some limitations like an unclear vision of the software product at the initial stage of the project and restricted involvement of external stakeholders as critical decision makers. However, with the integration of scrum and kanban with waterfall, the challenges of unclear product vision and restricted involvement of external stakeholders can be overcome (Bhavsar et al., 2020). The net result is an integration model using a mixture of traditional waterfall protocols with agility and workflow management. This disciplined and multi-method approach is being proposed in the quest to increase the likelihood of producing high-quality software products and achieve sustained competitive advantage.

## Technology

Technology plays a fundamental role in wealth creation, economic growth, improvement of the quality of life and the transformation of society. Science and technology can have a tremendous impact on economic development and digital transformation, as science and technology in combination are seen as knowing and applying specific knowledge to achieve efficiency, productivity, security, comfort and wealth.

The software development industry has been growing since the advent of the COVID-19 pandemic and the rise of automation technologies. This is so because many business processes can be automated, many daily tasks being executed by individuals can be automated and many project implementation tasks can be automated (Bhavsar et al., 2020). Both AI and ML have been assisting greatly in this area. Studies have found AI and ML are having a significant impact on the design, development and delivery of high-quality software products, based on their testing and defects detection abilities (Akinsanya et al., 2019). Thorough testing and effective flaw detection are critical because modern customers place a high demand on always being connected. There is also a high demand regarding the concept of 'always-on' mode in which they expect the features of software products to be working and operational at all times.

However, given the same requirements specification, different software development teams may take different approaches, thus leading to inappropriate use of development tools or non-optimized allocation of resources (Caldeira et al., 2019). Hence, one of the key challenges faced by software developers and project managers is to select the right software development approach, bearing in mind that no single approach is ideal to work optimally in all situations (Shaikh & Abro, 2019).

A critical question is whether small firms are willing and able to invest in and adopt AI and ML tools due to the advantage that they provide. The answer to this question is affirmative because the cost of these tools is reducing. In addition, open-source and proprietary software strategies are increasingly being employed by software development firms (Mens et al., 2019). However, significant disconnects may occur because the open-source community may be resistant to a company's involvement with prescribed policies and procedures. Such prescribed policies and procedures may be incompatible with the work practices of those in the open-source community, thus leading to communication and collaboration challenges.

### People

Contemporary software development has become much more social due to the large size, complexity and diversity of current software products (Mens et al., 2019). In general, current project tasks are performed by humans who are required to employ their subjective expertise, with the assistance of software development tools. The current trend is for innovators of technology and businessmen to come together as a unified force to develop and deploy software products. This union creates what is called 'technopreneurs'. A number of software products (Apps) are developed through this means.

Implementing software products is more than just getting the software to run. Implementing software in organizations can change business processes, as well as the way employees work and think (Orlikowski & Robey, 1991). Similarly, implementing software for individuals requires adherence to various quality dimensions like screen navigation (user interface), functionality, maintainability and usability. Hence, software development has political, social (people), cultural, legal and technical implications.

Technical issues are rarely the cause of project failures; the predominant cause is people.

It is believed that software success or failure is a direct consequence of the effectiveness of collaboration, expectation management and change management processes (Dwivedi et al., 2014), especially in this era of distributed teams. The utilization of distributed teams in software development requires active user/developer involvement, close cooperation and collaboration among all key stakeholders. It is felt that people are the main determinants of software project success, but they must be motivated and flexible (Tam et al., 2020). As a result, effective communication and continual interaction are critical during the development process, in an effort to deliver high-quality software products and successful projects.

The philosophy of the people-driven paradigm of software development states that "If the people on the project are good enough, they can use almost any process and accomplish their assignment. If they are not good enough, no process will repair their inadequacy" (Cockburn & Highsmith, 2001, p. 131).

However, it is important to note that there are people, financial and infrastructural constraints in developing economies, especially in the Caribbean. Such constraints can influence talented and capable software developers in developing economies to migrate to developed economies where the opportunities for growth and development are greater. This migration trend could be one of the reasons (factor) why the people construct was not found to be significant in relation to software product quality in Caribbean software development firms.

Another reason for the non-significance of people in the study could be information asymmetry as explained in the agency theory. When ownership and control are separated in the execution of projects, tension can occur between the project sponsor and the project manager/software developer (the agent). The underlying assumption of the agency theory is that the agent who is generally more knowledgeable than the project sponsor (the principal) is basically more concerned with his/her self-interest and unless monitored closely will exploit the project sponsor. Studies have found that close monitoring can lead to project success, but monitoring can increase the project cost. The condition of increased cost is difficult to find and be absorbed in small firms in developing economies.

In addition to people, the digital divide between developed and developing economies can be another cause of project failures. The Network Readiness Index and the Internet Penetration Rate highlight the potential challenges experienced in developing economies to adequately take advantage of information and communication technology (ICT) due to lack of access and lack of knowledge. Hence, it is reported that software projects in developing countries usually fail before being introduced (Badewi & Shehab, 2016). The good news is that the cost of software development is decreasing due to the proliferation of open-source software products and cloud services (Alvertis et al., 2016).

**Process Maturity**

Managing software quality is a major challenge for many software development firms. In an effort to overcome the challenge, many firms have adopted software process improvement (SPI) initiatives. However, small firms, especially those in developing economies, which are experiencing various financial and human constraints, find these SPI initiatives to be cumbersome, disruptive and costly, which by extension leads to low adoption. Notwithstanding, studies have demonstrated the benefits of these SPI initiatives, such as improved software product quality, improved software developer productivity, reduced project cycle time and improved customer satisfaction. The two case studies on Wipro Limited and Dynanet Corporation illustrate the benefits of adopting the CMMI along the quality improvement journey.

Starting a software development project from scratch is a complex process and so it is important to be guided by a process improvement framework like the Capability Maturity Model Integration (CMMI) with prescribed developmental practices. Inadequate and inaccurate project planning can cause substantial losses of financial, physical and human resources. Thus, understanding the developmental process is a major factor in improving the efficiency and effectiveness of software development projects (Caldeira et al., 2019).

The philosophy of the plan-driven paradigm of software development states that "everyone realizes the importance of having a motivated, quality work force and the latest technology, but even the finest people can't perform at their best when the process is not understood or operating at its best" (SEI, 2005, p. 9). Regardless of the capability of people and the maturity of the process, value can only be achieved by organizations and individuals when the software product is being used, at least its major features.

### The SPIM-S Framework

An exploratory sequential mixed methods study was taken to develop the SPIM-S framework. Initially, focus group sessions were held with software developers to determine the top 10 CMMI Level 2 and Level 3 process practices based on the constraints and norms in the Caribbean. Subsequent to the derived top 10 process practices, a survey was conducted among 112 software developer/user dyads. Upon completion of the analysis, based on the mean scores of the top 10 process practices, it is reasonable to conclude that software development firms in the Caribbean are operating at about CMMI Levels 2 and 3. Furthermore, only three out of ten process practices were found to be significant in relation to software product quality. The three process practices are organization process definition (OPD), organization process focus (OPF), and verification + validation (Ver+Val), all CMMI Level 3 practices. Based on this finding, key stakeholders (software developers, project managers and users) in the software development industry in the Caribbean need to attend seminars on the role and benefits of SPI and CMMI initiatives in order to increase the maturity of their software development process.

A continuous representation of the CMMI was taken in developing the SPIM-S framework. After the institutionalization of the three process practices that were found significant (OPD, OPF and Ver+Val), then other Levels 2 and 3 process practices will be incorporated into the model before the Level 4 and Level 5 process practices are included.

In addition, both process practices and technology were found to have a significant impact on software product quality. In the final analysis, the SPIM-S framework was validated with people, process practices and technology explaining 27.6% of the variance in software product quality. This means that there are other factors like culture, project size, team size and project complexity, accounting for 72.4% which could impact software product quality.

The SPIM-S is being proposed to increase the adoption of some form of SPI initiative by small firms. It is hoped that the adoption of this simplified model by small firms will be high because the SPIM-S will be viewed as a less disruptive and costly framework. It is felt that increased adoption can lead to higher software product quality which can lead to sustained competitive advantage.

### Future Research

Future research can improve the reporting and understanding of the phenomenon, which in this case is SPI and CMMI. It can address the effects of specific factors on the dependent variable, which in this case is software product quality. It is almost impossible for one study to address all the possible concerns of a phenomenon. Thus, future research can play an important role in discovering new insights. Future research can build upon the findings of prior studies, address the limitations of prior studies, replicate the same research in a new context, location or culture and expand a theory.

In addition, sometimes it is important to observe the impact of specific factors on the dependent variable over time to track changes and trends. This kind of research constitutes a longitudinal study. There is such appeal in the literature which states that there is a need for more longitudinal studies in the area of software development (Dwivedi et al., 2014). Because misalignment of software products has led to the bankruptcy of some firms, there is an appeal for longitudinal studies that can explain the processes by which misalignments between software projects and institutional practices are resolved.

Equally important is further study regarding which production method or hybrid technique is preferred under various contexts, as context matters in software development. More specifically, in regard to this study, the following could be explored.

1. Although the four Caribbean countries in this study constitute 83% of the Caribbean population, future research could include other Caribbean countries in the software development industry.

2. In addition to people, process and technology future research could include project team size and project complexity and their impact on software product quality. Team size refers to the number of persons on the project team. Team size can be classified as small, medium and large. Prior study has shown that small projects are more efficient in responding to changes (Lee & Xia, 2005). It is expected that smaller projects are likely to be more successful than larger projects (Standish Group, 2015).

A complex project is one that has a number of characteristics (level of severity), that makes it extremely difficult to predict project outcomes (Remington et al., 2009). Studies found that project complexity can negatively impact the success of projects (Luo et al., 2017; Muller et al., 2012; Standish Group, 2015).

3. Are small software development firms willing and able to invest in AI and ML bearing in mind the potential benefits of these development tools?

The debate continues regarding a unified definition/understanding of a successful project, even though the Standish Group has done an excellent job in this area. For example, how can one categorize a software project that is functionally brilliant but misses its cost or schedule targets by 10%? It is believed that literalists would categorize it as a failure, but realists would categorize it as a success (Glass, 2005). Another example is that software developers might assess a software project as a success, while users and top management might assess the same project as a failure (Dwivedi et al., 2014). This multi-perspective view on software development requires future research to evaluate the different views of the key stakeholders involved in the process.

### References

Akinsanya, B. J., Araujo, L. J., Charikova, M., Gimaeva, S., Grichshenko, A., Khan, A., & Shilintsev, D. (2019). Machine learning and value generation in software development: A survey. *Tools and Methods of Program Analysis*, *1288*, 44–55.

Alvertis, I., Koussouris, S., Papaspyros, D., Arvanitakis, E., Mouzakitis, S., Franken, S., & Prinz, W. (2016). User involvement is software development processes. *Procedia Computer Science*, *97*, 73–83.

Badewi, A., & Shehab, E. (2016). The impact of organizational project benefits management governance on ERP project success: Neo-institutional theory perspective. *International Journal of Project Management, 34*(3), 412–428.

Bhavsar, K., Shah, V., & Gopalan, S. (2020). Scrumbanfall: An agile integration of Scrum and Kanban with Waterfall in software engineering. *International Journal of Innovation Technology and Exploring Engineering, 9*(4), 2075–2084.

Caldeira, J., Abreu, F. B., Reis, J., Portugal, L., & Cardoso, J. (2019). *Assessing software development teams' efficiency using process mining*. Paper presented at the International Conference on Process Mining in Aachen, Germany, 65–72.

Chevers, D. A., Mills, A. M., Duggan, E., & Moore, S. (2020). A software process improvement model for small firms in developing countries. In Zuopeng (Justin) Zhang (Ed.), *Novel theories and applications of global information resource management* (pp. 47–80). Pennsylvania: IGI Global.

Cockburn, A., & Highsmith, J. (2001). Agile software development: The people factor. *Computer, 34*(11), 131–133.

Duggan, E. W. (2006). Tranquilizing the werewolf that attacks information systems quality. In Mehdi Khosrow-Pour (Ed.), *Advanced topics in information resources management* (pp. 253–281). Pennsylvania: IGI Global.

Dwivedi, Y. K., Wastell, D., Laumer, S., Henriksen, H. Z., Myers, M. D., Bunker, D., Elbana, A., Ravishankar, M. N., & Srivastava, S. C. (2014). Research on information systems failures and success: Status update and future directions. *Information System Frontier, 17*(1), 143–157.

Dwivedi, M., Yadav, A., & Venkatesh, U. (2012). Use of social media by national tourism organizations: A preliminary analysis. *Information Technology & Tourism, 13*, 1–10.

Glass, E. L. (2005). It failure rates: 70% or 10–15%? *IEEE Software, 22*(3), 110–112.

Heeks, R. (2002). Information systems and developing countries: Failure, success, and local improvisations. *The Information Society, 18*, 101–112.

Krasner, H. (2021). The cost of poor software quality in the US: A 2020 Report. *Consortium for Information and Software Quality*, 1–46.

Lee, G., & Xia, W. (2005). The ability of information systems development project teams to respond to business and technology changes: A study of flexibility measures. *European Journal of Information Systems, 14*, 75–92.

Luo, L., He, Q., Xie, J., Yang, D., & Wu, G. (2017). Investigating the relationship between project complexity and success in complex construction projects. *Journal of Management Engineering, 33*(2), 1–11.

Mens, T., Cataldo, M., & Damian, D. (2019). The social developer: The future of software development. *IEEE Software, 36*, 11–14.

Muller, R., Geraldi, J., & Turner, J. R. (2012). Relationship between leadership and success in different types of project complexities. *IEEE Transactions on Engineering Management, 59*(1), 77–90.

Orlikowski, W. J., & Robey, D. (1991). Information technology and the structuring of organizations. *Information Systems Research, 2*(2), 143–169.

Porter, M. (1985). *Competitive advantage*. New York: The Free Press.

Remington, K., Zolin, R., & Turner, R. (2009). *A model of project complexity: Distinguishing dimensions of complexity from severity*. Paper presented at the 9th International Research Network of Project Management Conference, Berlin.

SEI. (2005). Capability Maturity Model Integration (CMMI) version 1.1 Overview, 9. Retrieved from www.sei.cmu.edu/cmmi/adoption/pdf/cmmi-overview05.pdf.

Shaikh, S., & Abro, S. (2019). Comparison of traditional and agile software development methodology: A short survey. *International Journal of Software Engineering and Computer Systems*, 5(2), 1–14.

Standish Group, T. (2015). Standish group 2015 Chaos report. *The Standish Group*, 1–16.

Tam, C., Moura, E. J., Oliveira, T., & Varajao, J. (2020). The factors influencing the success of on-going agile software development projects. *International Journal of Project Management*, 38, 165–176.

# Index

Pages in *italics* refer to figures and **bold** refer to tables.